Towards a Sociology of the Novel

Lucien Goldmann

Towards a Sociology of the Novel

Translated from the French by Alan Sheridan

TAVISTOCK PUBLICATIONS

Originally published in French under the title
Pour une sociologie du roman
by Éditions Gallimard

© Éditions Gallimard 1964

This translation first published in Great Britain in 1975
by Tavistock Publications Limited
11 New Fetter Lane London EC4

© Tavistock Publications Limited 1975

SBN 422 74240 6

Typeset by
Preface Ltd, Salisbury, Wilts
and printed in Great Britain by
The Cambridge University Press

Contents

For Annie

Preface

The first three chapters of this book were published in a number of the *Revue de l'Institut de Sociologie de Bruxelles* (2:1963) devoted to the sociology of the novel. One of these, the study of the *nouveau roman* and social reality, is based on a paper given at a discussion in which Alain Robbe-Grillet and Nathalie Sarraute also took part — a number of points concerning the work of Robbe-Grillet were developed later. These three chapters are the result of two years of research on the sociology of the novel carried out at the Centre de Sociologie de la Littérature of the Institut de Sociologie de l'Université de Bruxelles.

The fourth chapter was written for the American review *Modern Language Notes*, in which it will probably be published at the same time as this book.

In this preface, I would simply like to anticipate a possible objection concerning the discrepancy between the levels on which the first and second chapters operate. The first is based on an entirely general hypothesis as to the correlation between the history of the novel form and the history of economic life in Western societies. The second chapter, on the other hand, is a very concrete study of the novels of André Malraux, in which I seldom go beyond internal structural analysis and in which the strictly sociological component is extremely limited. I should also add that the third chapter, the study of the *nouveau roman*, is situated at an intermediary level between the extreme generality of the first and the internal analysis of the second.

These differences of level are real enough and derive from the fact that, far from being a completed piece of research, this book presents only the partial results of a continuing process of research.

The sociological problems of the novel form are fascinating and extremely complex. They could also have a profound effect on both the sociology of culture and literary criticism. Furthermore, they cover a particularly wide field. That is why there can be no question of making progress solely through the efforts of a single researcher or of a number of researchers in one or two centres.

I shall try, of course, to continue my research both at the École Pratique des Hautes Études in Paris and at the Centre de Sociologie de la Littérature in Brussels. But I know that in the years to come I shall be able to cover only a small section of the immense field that remains to be explored. I am also well aware that really substantial progress will only be possible when the sociology of literature becomes a field of collective research carried out in a sufficiently large number of universities and research centres throughout the world.

It was from this point of view, and because the results already achieved, however partial and provisional, seemed to me to be important enough to throw a new light on the problem, that I decided to publish them. In doing so, I hope that they may be integrated into the work of other researchers, or, at least, considered and discussed by them. They may even, perhaps, stimulate research along similar lines. I also hope that sociological publications coming from other sources will subsequently help me in my own work.

In concluding this preface, I should like to emphasize once again the extent to which recent methods of literary criticism – genetic structuralism, psychoanalysis, and even static structuralism, to which I am opposed, but some of the partial results of which are of undoubted value – have at last established the need to constitute a serious, rigorous, and positive science of the life of the mind in general and of cultural creation in particular.

Of course, this science is still in its earliest stages. We possess few examples of concrete research, whereas, on the contrary, traditional studies – of an empirical, positivistic, or psychological kind – dominate university life throughout the world, at least from a quantitative point of view. It should be added that the few scientific works that exist are particularly unapproachable for the general reader, and even for the student, in so far as they run counter to a whole series of firmly entrenched mental habits, while traditional studies, are, on the contrary, favoured by these habits and, therefore, easily approachable. This is because, in the scientific study of cultural life, we are concerned with changes of a *radical* kind, similar to those that made possible the constitution of the positive sciences of nature.

What, in effect, appeared to be more absurd than to affirm the rotation of the earth or the principle of inertia when everyone could certify by immediate and unchallengeable experience that the earth did not move and that a stone never continued its trajectory indefinitely? What seems more absurd today than the affirmation that the true subjects of cultural creation are social groups and not isolated individuals, when immediate and apparently unchallengeable experience tells us that every cultural work – whether literary, artistic, or philosophical – has an individual as its author?

But science has always been constituted in the face of 'immediate evidence' and 'common sense'; and this constitution has always come up against the same difficulties, the same resistances, and the same types of argument.

This is normal enough and even, in the final resort, encouraging and positive. It proves that through resistances and obstacles, in the face of conformism and intellectual cowardliness, scientific work continues on its way, slowly no doubt, but nevertheless effectively.

Paris, June 1964

I have taken the opportunity of a reprinting of this book to add three notes (pp. 124, 145 note 6, 167) and a study of Robbe-Grillet's latest film (written in collaboration with Anne Olivier and published in *L'Observateur* on September 18, 1964).

It should be added that the affirmation that 'the true subjects of cultural creation are social groups and not isolated individuals' was not taken kindly by the critics. It was written in order to provoke discussion and I readily acknowledge today that its perhaps over-elliptical form might have encouraged misunderstanding.

However, I had explained my position at length in previous works. The remarks that I have added to the last chapter of this book will do much to clear up the matter. Nevertheless, I still believe, in the sense in which Hegel wrote that 'the True is the All', that the true subjects of cultural creation are, in fact, social groups and not isolated individuals; but the individual creator belongs to the group, often by birth or social position, always by virtue of the objective signification of his work, and occupies in the group a place that may not be decisive, but is certainly privileged.

In so far as *the tendency to coherence that constitutes the essence of the work is situated not only at the level of the individual creator, but already at that of the group*, the approach by which this group is seen as the true subject of creation may account for the role of the writer and integrate him in its analysis, *whereas the reverse does not appear to be the case*.

Paris, April 1965

1 Introduction to the Problems of a Sociology of the Novel

Two years ago, in January 1961, the Institute of Sociology in the Free University of Brussels asked me to lead a research group into the sociology of literature, beginning with the novels of André Malraux. With a good deal of apprehension, I accepted. My work on seventeenth-century philosophy and tragedy in no way prejudiced me against the possibility of a similar study of the novel, even of a body of fiction so nearly contemporary as Malraux's. In fact, we spent the first year on a preliminary study of the problems of the novel as a literary form, taking as our starting-point Georg Lukács's already almost classic work – though still little known in France – *The Theory of the Novel*[1] and René Girard's recently published *Mensonge romantique et vérité romanesque*,[2] in which Girard – unknown to himself, as he later told me – discovered the Lukácsian analyses, while modifying them on several particular points.

Our study of *The Theory of the Novel* and Girard's book led me to formulate a number of sociological hypotheses that seem to me to be particularly interesting, and on the basis of which my later work on Malraux's novels was developed.

These hypotheses concern, on the one hand, the homology between the structure of the classical novel and the structure of exchange in the liberal economy and, on the other hand, certain parallels in their later evolutions.

Let us begin by tracing the outlines of the structure described by Lukács. This structure may not, as he believed, characterize the novel form in general, but it does characterize at least its most important aspects (and probably, from the genetic point of view, its primordial aspect). The novel form studied by Lukács is that characterized by a hero that he very felicitously calls the *problematic hero*.[3]

The novel is the story of a *degraded* (what Lukács calls 'demoniacal') search, a search for authentic values in a world itself degraded, but at an otherwise advanced level according to a different mode.

By authentic values, I mean, of course, not the values that the critic or the reader regards as authentic, but those which, without being manifestly present in the novel, organize in accordance with an *implicit* mode its world as a whole. It goes without saying that these values are specific to each novel and different from one novel to another.

Since the novel is an epic genre characterized, unlike the folk tale or the epic poem itself, by the insurmountable rupture between the hero and the world, there is in Lukács an analysis of the nature of two degradations (that of the hero and that of the world) that must engender both a *constitutive opposition*, the foundation of this insurmountable rupture, and an *adequate community* to make possible the existence of an epic form.

The radical rupture alone would, in effect, have led to tragedy or to lyric poetry; the absence of rupture or the existence of a merely accidental rupture would have led to the epic poem or the folk tale.

Situated between the two, the novel has a dialectical nature in so far as it derives specifically, on the one hand, from the fundamental community of the hero and of the world presupposed by all epic forms and, on the other hand, from their insurmountable rupture; the community of the hero and of the world resulting from the fact that they are both degraded in relation to authentic values, the opposition resulting from the difference of nature between each of these two degradations.

The *demoniacal* hero of the novel is a madman or a criminal, in any case, as I have said, a *problematic* character whose degraded, and therefore inauthentic, search for authentic values in a world of conformity and convention constitute the content of this new literary genre known as the 'novel' that writers created in an individualistic society.

On the basis of this analysis, Lukács develops a typology of the novel. Setting out from the relation between the hero and the world, he distinguishes three schematic types of the Western novel in the nineteenth century, to which is added a fourth that already constitutes a transformation from the novel form towards new modalities that would require a different type of analysis. In 1920, this fourth possibility seemed to him to be expressed pre-eminently in the novels of Tolstoy, which strive towards the epic. The three types of novel on which his analysis bears are as follows:

a)   the novel of 'abstract idealism'; characterized by the activity of the hero and by his over-narrow consciousness in relation to the complexity of the world (*Don Quixote, Le Rouge et le Noir*);

b)   the psychological novel; concerned above all with the analysis of the inner life, and characterized by the passivity of the hero and a consciousness too broad to be satisfied by what the world of convention can offer him (*Oblomov* and *L'Éducation sentimentale*);

c)   the *Bildungsroman*, which ends with a *self-imposed limitation*; although the hero gives up the problematic search, he does not accept the world of convention or abandon the implicit scale of values – a self-imposed limitation that must be characterized by the term 'virile maturity' (Goethe's *Wilhelm Meister* or Gottfried Keller's *Der grüne Heinrich*).

At a distance of forty years, René Girard's analyses are often very close to those of Lukács. For Girard, too, the novel is the story of a degraded search (which he calls 'idolatrous') for authentic values, by a problematic hero, in a degraded world. The terminology he uses is Heideggerian in origin, but he often gives it a content that is somewhat different from that of Heidegger himself. Without going into detail, we might say that Girard replaces Heidegger's duality of the ontological and the ontic by the obviously related duality of the ontological and the metaphysical, which correspond for him to the authentic and the inauthentic; but whereas, for Heidegger, any idea of progress and retreat is to be eliminated, Giarard confers on his terminology of the ontological and the metaphysical a content much closer to the positions of Lukács than to those of Heidegger, by introducing between the two terms a relation governed by the categories of progress and regression.[4]

Girard's typology of the novel is based on the idea that the degradation of the fictional world is the result of a more or less advanced ontological sickness (this 'more or less' is strictly contrary to Heidegger's thinking) to which corresponds, within the fictional world, an increase of metaphysical desire, that is to say, of degraded desire.

It is based therefore on the idea of degradation, and it is here that Girard introduces into the Lukácsian analysis a precision that seems to me particularly important. For him, indeed, the degradation of the fictional world, the progress of the ontological sickness, and the increase of metaphysical desire are expressed in a greater or lesser *mediatization* that progressively increases the distance between metaphysical desire and authentic search, the search for 'vertical transcendence'.

There are a great many examples of mediation in Girard's work, from the novels of chivalry that stand between *Don Quixote* and the search for chivalric values to the lover that stands between the husband and his desire for his wife, in Dostoievsky's *The Eternal Husband*. Incidentally, it does not seem to me that his examples are always as well chosen. Moreover, I am not at all sure that mediatization is as universal a category in the fictional world as Girard thinks. The term 'degradation' seems to me broader and more appropriate, on condition of course that the nature of this degradation is specified in each particular analysis.

Nevertheless, by introducing the category of mediation, and even by exaggerating its importance, Girard has elucidated the analysis of a structure that involved not only the most important form of degradation in the fictional world but also the form that is, from a genetic point of view, probably the first, that which gave birth to the literary genre of the novel, the novel itself having emerged as the result of other derived forms of degradation.

From this point on, Girard's typology is based first of all on the existence of two forms of mediation, external and internal, the first characterized by the fact that the mediating agent is external to the world in which the hero's search takes place (for example, the novels of chivalry in *Don Quixote*), the second by the fact that the mediating agent belongs to this world (the lover in *The Eternal Husband*).

Within these two qualitatively different groups, there is the idea of a progressive degradation that is expressed by the increasing proximity between the fictional character and the mediating agent, and the increasing distance between this character and *vertical transcendence.*

Let us now try to elucidate an essential point on which Lukács and Girard are in fundamental disagreement. As the story of a degraded search for authentic values in an inauthentic world, the novel is necessarily both a biography and a social chronicle. A particularly important fact is that the situation of the writer in relation to the world he has created is, in the novel, different from the situation in relation to the world of any other literary form. This particular situation, Girard calls *humour*; Lukács calls it *irony.* Both agree that the novelist must supersede the consciousness of his heroes and that this supersession (humour or irony) is aesthetically constitutive of fictional creation. But they diverge as to the nature of this supersession and, on this point, it is the position of Lukács that seems to me to be acceptable and not that of Girard.

For Girard, the novelist has left the world of degradation and rediscovered authenticity, vertical transcendence, at the moment he writes his work. This is why he thinks that most great novels end with a conversion of the hero to this vertical transcendence and that the abstract character of certain endings (*Don Quixote, Le Rouge et le Noir*, one might also add *La Princesse de Clèves*) is either an illusion on the part of the reader, or the result of survivals from the past in the consciousness of the writer.

Such a notion is strictly contrary to Lukács's aesthetic, for which any *literary form* (and any great artistic form in general) is born out of the need to express an *essential* content. If the fictional degradation were really superseded by the writer, even through the ultimate conversion of a number of heroes, the story of this degradation would be no more than a mere incident and its expression would have at most the character of a more or less entertaining narrative.

And yet the writer's irony, his autonomy in relation to his characters, the ultimate conversion of the fictional heroes are undoubted realities.

However, Lukács thinks that precisely to the extent that the novel is the imaginary creation of a world governed by *universal* degradation, this supersession cannot itself be other than degraded, *abstract*, conceptual, and not experienced as a concrete reality.

According to Lukács the novelist's irony is directed not only on to the hero, whose demoniacal character he is well aware of, but also on the abstract, and therefore inadequate and degraded, character of his own consciousness. That is why the story of the degraded search, whether demoniacal or idolatrous, always remains the sole way of expressing essential realities.

The ultimate conversion of Don Quixote or Julien Sorel is not, as Girard believes, a discovery of authenticity, vertical transcendence, but simply an awareness of the vanity, the degraded character not only of the earlier search, but also of any hope, of any possible search.

That is why it is an end and not a beginning and it is the existence of this irony (which is always a self-irony, as well) that enables Lukács to make two related definitions that seem to me particularly appropriate to this form of the novel: *the Way is begun, the journey is ended*, and *the novel is the form of virile maturity*, the second formula defining more specifically, as we have seen, the *Bildungsroman* of the *Wilhelm Meister* type, which ends with a self-imposed limitation (the hero gives up the problematic search, without accepting the world of convention or abandoning the explicit scale of values).

Thus the novel, in the sense given it by Lukács and Girard, appears as a literary genre in which authentic values, which are always involved, cannot be present in the work in the form of conscious characters or concrete realities. These values exist only in an abstract, conceptual form in the consciousness of the novelist in which they take on an *ethical* character. But abstract ideas have no place in a literary work, where they would form a heterogeneous element.

The problem of the novel, therefore, is to make what in the novelist's consciousness is *abstract* and *ethical* the essential element of a work in which reality can exist only in the mode of a non-thematized (Girard would say mediatized) absence or, which is equivalent, a degraded presence. As Lukács says, the novel is the only literary genre in which *the novelist's ethic becomes an aesthetic problem of the work.*

The problem of a sociology of the novel has always preoccupied sociologists of literature, though, as yet, no decisive step towards its elucidation has so far been attempted. Basically, the novel, for the first part of its history, was a biography and a social chronicle and so it has always been possible to show that the social chronicle reflected to a greater or lesser degree the society of the period — and one does not have to be a sociologist to see that.

On the other hand, a connection has also been made between the transformation of the novel since Kafka and the Marxist analyses of reification. Here, too, it has to be said that serious sociologists should have seen this as a problem rather than as an explanation. Although it is obvious that the absurd worlds of Kafka or Camus's *L'Étranger*, or Robbe-Grillet's world composed of relatively autonomous objects, correspond to the analysis of reification as developed by Marx and later Marxists, the problem arises as to why, when this analysis was elaborated in the second half of the nineteenth century and concerned a phenomenon that appeared in a still earlier period, this same phenomenon was expressed in the novel only at the end of World War I.

In short, all these analyses concern the relation between certain elements of the *content* of fictional literature and the existence of a social reality that they reflect almost without transposition or by means of a more or less transparent transposition.

But the first problem that a sociology of the novel should have confronted is that of the relation between the *novel form* itself and the *structure* of the social environment in which it developed, that is to say, between the novel as a literary genre and individualistic modern society.

It seems to me today that a combination of the analyses of Lukács and Girard, even though they were both developed without specifically sociological preoccupations, makes it possible, if not to elucidate this problem entirely, at least to make a decisive step towards its elucidation.

I have just said that the novel can be characterized as the story of a search for authentic values in a degraded mode, in a degraded society, and that this degradation, in so far as it concerns the hero, is expressed principally through the mediatization, the reduction of authentic values to the implicit level and their disappearance as manifest realities. This is obviously a particularly complex structure and it would be difficult to imagine that it could one day emerge simply from individual invention without any basis in the social life of the group.

What, however, would be quite inconceivable, is that a literary form of such dialectical complexity should be rediscovered, over a period of centuries, among the most different writers in the most varied countries, that it should have become the form *par excellence* in which was expressed, on the literary plane, the content of a whole period, without there being either a homology or a significant relation between this form and the most important aspects of social life.

This hypothesis seems to me particularly simple and above all productive and credible, though it has taken me years to find it.

The novel form seems to me, in effect, to be *the transposition on the literary plane of everyday life in the individualistic society created by market production.* There is a *rigorous homology* between the literary form of the novel, as I have defined it with the help of Lukács and Girard, and the everyday relation between man and commodities in general, and by extension between men and other men, in a market society.

The natural, healthy relation between men and commodities is that in which production is consciously governed by future consumption, by the concrete qualities of objects, by their *use value.*

Now what characterizes market production is, on the contrary, the elimination of this relation with men's consciousness, its reduction to the implicit through the mediation of the new economic reality created by this form of production: *exchange value.*

In other forms of society, when a man needed an article of clothing or a house, he had to produce them himself or obtain them from someone capable of producing them and who was under an obligation to provide him with them, either in accordance with certain traditional rules, or for reasons of authority, friendship, etc., or as part of some reciprocal arrangement.[5]

If one wishes to obtain an article of clothing or a house today, one has to find the money needed to buy them. The producer of clothes or houses is indifferent to the use values of the objects he produces. For him, these objects are no more than a necessary evil to obtain what alone interests him, an exchange value sufficient to ensure the viability of his enterprise. In the economic life, which constitutes the most important part of modern social life, every authentic relation with the qualitative aspect of objects and persons tends to disappear — interhuman relations as well as those between men and things — and be replaced by a mediatized and degraded relation: the relation with purely quantitative exchange values.

Of course, use values continue to exist and even to govern, in the last resort, the whole of the economic life; but their action assumes an *implicit character, exactly like that of authentic values in the fictional world.*

On the conscious, manifest plane, *the economic life* is composed of people orientated exclusively towards exchange values, degraded values, to which are added in production a number of individuals – the creators in every sphere – who remain essentially orientated towards use values and who by virtue of that fact are situated on the fringes of society and become *problematic individuals*; and, of course, even these individuals unless they accept the romantic illusion (Girard would say lie) of the *total* rupture between essence and appearance, between the inner life and the social life, cannot be deluded as to the degradations that their creative activity undergoes in a market society, when this activity is manifested externally, when it becomes a book, a painting, teaching, a musical composition, etc., enjoying a certain prestige, and having therefore a certain price. It should be added that as the ultimate consumer, opposed in the very act of exchange to the producers, any individual in a market society finds himself at certain moments of the day aiming at qualitative use values that he can obtain only through the mediation of exchange values.

In view of this, there is nothing surprising about the creation of the novel as a literary genre. Its apparently extremely complex form is the one in which men live every day, when they are obliged to seek all quality, all use value in a mode degraded by the mediation of quantity, of exchange value – and this in a society in which any effort to orientate oneself *directly* towards use value can only produce individuals who are themselves degraded, but in a different mode, that of *the problematic individual.*

Thus the two structures, that of an important fictional genre and that of exchange proved to be strictly homologous, to the point at which one might speak of one and the same structure manifesting itself on two different planes. Furthermore, as we shall see later, the *evolution* of the fictional form that corresponds to the world of reification can be understood only in so far as it is related to a *homologous history* of the structure of reification.

However, before making a few remarks about this homology between the two evolutions we must examine the problem, particularly important for the sociologist, of the process by which the literary form was able to emerge out of the economic reality, and of the modifications that the study of this process forces us to introduce into the traditional representation of the sociological conditioning of literary creation.

One fact is striking at the outset; the traditional scheme of literary sociology, whether Marxist or not, cannot be applied in the case of the structural homology just referred to. Most work in the sociology of literature established a relation between the most important literary works and the collective *consciousness* of the particular social group from which they emerged. On this point, the traditional Marxist position does not differ essentially from non-Marxist sociological work as a whole, in relation to which it introduces only four new ideas, namely:

a)   The literary work is not the mere reflection of a real, given collective consciousness, but the culmination at a very advanced level of coherence of tendencies peculiar to the consciousness of a particular group, a consciousness that must be conceived as a dynamic reality, orientated towards a certain state of equilibrium. What really separates, in this as in all other spheres, Marxist sociology from positivistic, relativist, or eclectic sociological tendencies is the fact that it sees the key concept not in the *real* collective consciousness, but in the constructed concept (*zugerechnet*) of *possible consciousness* which, alone, makes an understanding of the first possible.

b)   The relation between collective ideology and great individual literary, philosophical, theological etc. creations resides not in an identity of content, but in a more advanced coherence and in a homology of structures, which can be expressed in imaginary contents very different from the real content of the collective consciousness.

c)   The work corresponding to the mental structure of the particular social group may be elaborated in certain exceptional cases by an individual with very few relations with this group. The *social* character of the work resides above all in the fact that an individual can never establish by himself a coherent mental structure corresponding to what is called a 'world view'. Such a structure can be elaborated only by a group, the individual being capable only of carrying it to a very high degree of coherence and transposing it on the level of imaginary creation, conceptual thought, etc.

d)   The collective consciousness is neither a primary reality, nor an autonomous reality; it is elaborated implicitly in the over-all behaviour of individuals participating in the economic, social, political life, etc.

These are evidently extremely important theses, sufficient to establish a very great difference between Marxist thinking and other conceptions of the sociology of literature. Nevertheless, despite these differences, Marxist theoreticians, like positivistic or relativistic sociologists of literature, have always thought that the social life can be expressed on the literary, artistic, or philosophical plane only through the intermediary link of the collective consciousness.

In the case we have just studied, however, what strikes one first is the fact that although we find a strict homology between the structures of economic life and a certain particularly important manifestation, one can detect no analogous structure at the level of the *collective consciousness* that seemed hitherto to be the indispensable intermediary link to realize either the homology or an intelligible, significant relation between the different aspects of social existence.

The novel analysed by Lukács and Girard no longer seems to be the imaginary transposition of the *conscious structures* of a particular group, but seems to express on the contrary (and this may be the case of a very large part of modern art in general) a search for values that no social group defends effectively and that the economic life tends to make implicit in all members of the society.

The old Marxist thesis whereby the proletariat was seen as the only social group capable of constituting the basis of a new culture, by virtue of the fact that it was not integrated into the reified society, set out from the traditional sociological representation that presupposed that all authentic, important cultural creation could emerge only from a fundamental harmony between the mental structure of the creator and that of a partial group of relative size, but universal ambition. In reality, for Western society at least, the Marxist analysis has proved inadequate; the Western proletariat, far from remaining alien to the reified society and opposing it as a revolutionary force, has on the contrary become integrated into it to a large degree, and its trade union and political action, far from overthrowing this society and replacing it by a socialist world, has enabled it to gain a relatively better place in it than Marx's analysis foresaw.

Furthermore, cultural creation, although increasingly threatened by the reified society, has continued to flourish. Fictional literature, as perhaps modern poetic creation and contemporary painting, are authentic forms of cultural creation even though they cannot be attached to the consciousness – even a potential one – of a particular social group.

Before embarking on a study of the processes that made possible and produced this *direct* transposition of the economic life into the literary life, we should perhaps remark that although such a process seems contrary to the whole tradition of Marxist studies of cultural creation, it confirms nevertheless, in a quite unexpected way, one of the most important Marxist analyses of bourgeois thought, namely the theory of the fetishization of merchandise and reification. This analysis, which Marx regarded as one of his most important discoveries, affirms in effect that in market societies (that is to say, in types of society in which economic activity predominates), the collective consciousness gradually loses all active reality and tends to become a mere reflection[6] of the economic life and, ultimately, to disappear.

There was obviously, therefore, between this *particular* analysis of Marx and the general theory of literary and philosophical creation of later Marxists, who presupposed an active role of the collective consciousness, not a contradiction but an incoherence. The latter theory never envisaged the consequences for the sociology of literature of Marx's belief that there survives in market societies a radical modification of the status of the individual and collective consciousness and, implicitly, relations between the infrastructure and the superstructure. The analysis of reification elaborated first by Marx on the level of everyday life, then developed by Lukács in the field of philosophical, scientific, and political thought, finally taken up by a number of theoreticians in various specific domains, and about which I have myself published a study, would appear therefore, for the moment at least, to be confirmed by the facts in the sociological analysis of a certain fictional form.

Having said this, the question arises as to how the link between the economic structures and literary manifestations is made in a society in which this link occurs *outside the collective consciousness.*

With regard to this I have formulated the hypothesis of the convergent action of four different factors, namely:

a) The birth in the thinking of members of bourgeois society, on the basis of economic behaviour and the existence of exchange value, of the *category of mediation* as a fundamental and increasingly developed form of thought, with an implicit tendency to replace this thought by a total false consciousness in which the mediating value becomes an absolute value and in which the mediated value disappears entirely or, to put it more clearly, with the tendency to conceive of the access to all values from the point of view of mediation, together with a propensity to make of money and social prestige absolute values and not merely mediations that provide access to other values of a qualitative character.

b) The survival in this society of a number of individuals who are essentially *problematic* in so far as their thinking and behaviour remain dominated by qualitative values, even though they are unable to extract themselves entirely from the existence of the degrading mediation whose action permeates the whole of the social structure.

These individuals include, above all, the creators, writers, artists, philosophers, theologians, men of action, etc., whose thought and behaviour are governed above all by the quality of their work even though they cannot escape entirely from the action of the market and from the welcome extended them by the reified society.

c)   Since no important work can be the expression of a purely individual experience, it is likely that the novel genre could emerge and be developed only in so far as a *non-conceptualized*, affective discontent, an affective aspiration towards qualitative values, was developed either in society as a whole, or perhaps solely among the middle strata from which most novelists have come.[7]

d)   Lastly, in the liberal market societies, there was a set of values, which, though not trans-individual, nevertheless, had a universal aim and, within these societies, a general validity. These were the values of liberal individualism that were bound up with the very existence of the competitive market (in France, liberty, equality, and property, in Germany, *Bildungsideal*, with their derivatives, tolerance, the rights of man, development of the personality, etc.). On the basis of these values, there developed the category of *individual* biography that became the constitutive element of the novel. Here, however, it assumed the form of the *problematic* individual, on the basis of the following:

1. the personal experience of the problematic individuals mentioned above under *b*);
2. the internal contradiction between individualism as a universal value produced by bourgeois society and the important and painful limitations that this society itself brought to the possibilities of the development of the individual.

This hypothetical schema seems to me to be confirmed among other things by the fact that, when one of these four elements, individualism, has gradually been eliminated by the transformation of the economic life and the replacement of the economy of free competition by an economy of cartels and monopolies (a transformation that began at the end of the nineteenth century, but whose qualitative turning-point most economists would place between 1900 and 1910), we witness a parallel transformation of the novel form that culminates in the gradual dissolution and disappearance of the individual character, of the hero; a transformation that seems to me to be characterized in an extremely schematic way by the existence of two periods:

a)   The first, transitional period, during which the disappearance of the importance of the individual brings with it attempts to replace biography as the content of the work of fiction with values produced by different ideologies. For although, in Western societies, these values have proved to be too weak to produce their own literary forms, they might well give a new lease of life to an already existing form that was losing its former content. First and foremost, on this level, are the ideas of community and collective reality (institutions, family, social group, revolution, etc.) that had been introduced and developed in Western thinking by the socialist ideology.

b)   The second period, which begins more or less with Kafka and continues to the contemporary *nouveau roman*, and which has not yet come to an end, is characterized by an abandonment of any attempt to replace the problematic hero and individual biography by another reality and by the effort to write the novel of the absence of the subject, of the non-existence of any ongoing search.[8]

It goes without saying that this attempt to safeguard the novel form by giving it a content, related no doubt to the content of the traditional novel (it had always been the literary form of the problematic search and the absence of positive values), but nevertheless essentially different (it now involves the elimination of two essential elements of the specific content of the novel: the psychology of the problematic hero and the story of his demoniacal search), was to produce at the same time parallel orientations towards different forms of expression. There may be here elements for a sociology of the theatre of absence (Beckett, Ionesco, Adamov during a certain period) and also of certain aspects of non-figurative painting.

Lastly, we should mention a problem that might and ought to be the subject of later research. The novel form that we have just studied is essentially critical and oppositional. It is a form of resistance to developing bourgeois society. An individual resistance that can fall back, within a group, only on *affective* and *non-conceptualized* psychical processes precisely because conscious resistances that might have elaborated literary forms implying the possibility of a positive hero (in the first place, a proletarian oppositional consciousness such as Marx had hoped for and predicted) had not become sufficiently developed in Western societies. The novel with a problematic hero thus proves, contrary to traditional opinion, to be a literary form bound up certainly with history and the development of the bourgeoisie, but not the expression of the real or possible consciousness of that class.

But the problem remains as to whether, parallel with this literary form, there did not develop other forms that might correspond to the conscious values and effective aspirations of the bourgeoisie; and, on this point, I should like to mention, merely as a general and hypothetical suggestion, the possibility that the work of Balzac — whose structure ought, indeed, to be analysed from this point of view — might constitute the only great literary expression of the world as structured by the conscious values of the bourgeoisie: individualism, the thirst for power, money, and eroticism, which triumph over the ancient feudal values of altruism, charity, and love.

Sociologically, this hypothesis, if it proves to be correct, might be related to the fact that the work of Balzac is situated precisely at a period in which individualism, ahistorical in itself, structured the consciousness of a bourgeoisie that was in the process of constructing a new society and found itself at the highest and most intense level of its real historical efficacity.

We should also ask ourselves why, with the exception of this single case, this form of fictional literature had only a secondary importance in the history of Western culture, why the real consciousness and aspirations of the bourgeoisie never succeeded again, in the course of the nineteenth and twentieth centuries, in creating a literary form of its own that might be situated on the same level as the other forms that constitute the Western literary tradition.

On this point, I would like to make a few general hypotheses. The analysis that I have just developed extends to one of the most important novel forms a statement that now seems to me to be valid for almost all forms of *authentic cultural creation*. In relation to this statement the only expression that I could see for the moment was constituted precisely by the work of Balzac[9], who was able to create a great literary universe structured by purely individualistic values, at a historical moment when, concurrently, men animated by ahistorical values were accomplishing a considerable historical upheaval (an upheaval that was not really completed in France until the end of the bourgeois revolution in 1848). With this single exception (but perhaps one should add a few other possible exceptions that may have escaped my attention), it seems to me that there is valid literary and artistic creation only when there is an aspiration to transcendence on the part of the individual and a search for qualitative trans-individual values. 'Man passes beyond man,' I have written, slightly altering Pascal. This means that man can be authentic only in so far as he conceives himself or feels himself as part of a developing whole and situates himself in a historical or transcendent trans-individual dimension. But bourgeois ideology, bound up like bourgeois society itself with the existence of economic activity, is precisely the first ideology in history that is both radically profane and ahistorical; the first ideology whose tendency is to deny anything sacred, whether the otherworldly sacredness of the transcendent religions or the immanent sacredness of the historical future. It is, it seems to me, the fundamental reason why bourgeois society created the first radically nonaesthetic form of consciousness. The essential character of bourgeois ideology, rationalism, ignores in its extreme expressions the very existence of art. There is no Cartesian or Spinozian aesthetics, or even an aesthetics for Baumgarten — art is merely an inferior form of knowledge.

It is no accident therefore if, with the exception of a few particular situations, we do not find any great literary manifestations of the bourgeois consciousness itself. In a society bound up with the market, the artist is, as I have already said, a problematic individual, and this means a critical individual, opposed to society.

Nevertheless reified bourgeois ideology had its thematic values, values that were sometimes authentic, such as those of individualism, sometimes purely conventional, which Lukács called false consciousness and, in their extreme forms, bad faith, and Heidegger's 'chatter'. These stereotypes, whether authentic or conventional, thematized in the collective consciousness, were later able to produce, side by side with the authentic novel form, a parallel literature that also recounted an individual history and, naturally enough, since conceptualized values were involved, could depict a positive hero.

It would be interesting to follow the meanderings of the secondary novel forms that might be based, quite naturally, on the collective consciousness. One would end up perhaps — I have not yet made such a study — with a very varied spectrum, from the lowest forms of the Delly type to the highest forms to be found perhaps in such writers as Alexandre Dumas or Eugène Sue. It is also perhaps on this plane that we should situate, parallel with the *nouveau roman*, certain best-sellers that are bound up with the new forms of collective consciousness.

However, the extremely schematic sketch that I have just traced seems to me to provide a framework for a sociological study of the novel form. Such a study would be all the more important in that, apart from its own object, it would constitute a not inconsiderable contribution to the study of the psychical structures of certain social groups, the middle strata in particular.

NOTES AND REFERENCES

1   Georg Lukács, *The Theory of the Novel* (1971) (trans.,
     A. Bostock) London: Merlin Press.
2   René Girard, *Mensonge romantique et vérité romanesque* (1961)
     Paris: Grasset.
3   I should say however that, in my opinion, the field of validity of
     this hypothesis must be contracted, for, although the hypothesis
     may be applied to such important works in the history of literature

as Cervantes' *Don Quixote*, Stendhal's *Le Rouge et le Noir*, and
Flaubert's *Madame Bovary* and *L'Éducation sentimentale*, it can be
applied only very partially to *La Chartreuse de Parme* and not at all
to the works of Balzac, which occupy a considerable place in the
history of the Western novel. As such, however, Lukács's analyses
enable us, it seems to me, to undertake a serious sociological study
of the novel form.

4   In Heidegger's thinking, as indeed in that of Lukács, there is a
radical break between Being (For Lukács, Totality) and whatever
may be spoken of in the indicative (a judgement of fact), or in the
imperative (a judgement of value).

It is this difference that Heidegger designates as that of the
ontological and the ontic. And, from this point of view,
metaphysics, which is one of the highest and most general forms of
thought in the indicative, remains in the final resort in the domain
of the ontic.

While agreeing on the necessary distinction between the
ontological and the ontic, totality and the theoretical, the moral
and the metaphysical, the positions of Heidegger and Lukács are
essentially different in the way these relations are conceived.

As a philosophy of history, Lukács's thought implies the idea of
a coming-into-being (*devenir*) of knowledge, of a hope in progress,
and a risk of regression. Now, for him, progress is the bringing
together of positive thought and the category of totality;
regression, the distancing of these two, ultimately inseparable,
elements. The task of philosophy is precisely to introduce the
category of totality as the basis of all partial research and of all
reflection on positive data.

Heiddeger, on the other hand, establishes a radical separation
(and, by the very fact, an abstract and conceptual one) between
Being and the datum, between the ontological and the ontic,
between philosophy and positive science, thus eliminating any idea
of progress and regression. He, too, arrives in the end at a
philosophy of history, but it is an abstract philosophy with two
dimensions, the authentic and the inauthentic, openness to Being
and oblivion of Being.

So, although Girard's terminology is Heideggerian in origin, the
introduction of the catogories of progress and regression brings him
closer to Lukács.

5   While ever exchange remains *sporadic* because it bears solely on
surpluses or because it has the character of an exchange of use
values that individuals or groups cannot produce within an
essentially natural economy, the mental structure of mediation
does not appear or remains secondary. The fundamental
transformation in the development of reification results from the
advent of *market production*.

6   I speak of a 'consciousness-reflection' when the content of this
consciousness and the set of relations between the different
elements of the content (what I call its structure) undergo the
action of certain other domains of the social life, without acting in

turn on them. In practice, this situation has probably never been reached in capitalist society. This society creates, however, a tendency to the rapid and gradual diminution of the action of consciousness on the economic life and, conversely, to a continual increase of the action of the economic sector of the social life on the content and structure of consciousness.

7   There arises a problem here that is difficult to solve at the moment, but which might one day be solved by concrete sociological research. I mean the problem of the collective, affective, non-conceptualized 'sound-box' that made possible the development of the novel form.

Initially, I thought that reification, while tending to dissolve and to integrate in the over-all society different partial groups, and, therefore, to deprive them to a certain extent of their specificity, had a character so contrary to both the biological and psychological reality of the individual human being that it could not fail to engender in *all* individual human beings, to a greater or lesser degree, reactions of opposition (or, if this reification becomes degraded in a qualitatively more advanced way, to reactions of evasion), thus creating a diffuse resistance to the reified world, a resistance that would constitute the background of fictional creation.

Later, however, it seemed to me that this hypothesis contained an unproved *a priori* supposition: that of the existence of a biological nature whose external manifestations could not be entirely denatured by social reality.

In fact, it is just as likely that resistances, even affective ones, to reification are circumscribed within certain particular social strata, which positive research ought to delimit.

8   Lukács characterized the time of the traditional novel by the proposition: 'We have started on our way, our journey is over.' One might characterize the new novel by the suppression of the first half of this statement. Its time might be characterized by the statement: 'The aspiration is there, but the journey is over' (Kafka, Nathalie Sarraute), or simply by the observation that 'the journey is already over, though we never started on our way' (Robbe-Grillet's first three novels).

9   A year ago, when dealing with the same problems and mentioning the existence of the novel with a problematic hero and of a fictional sub-literature with a positive hero, I wrote, 'Lastly, I shall conclude this article with a great question mark, that of the sociological study of the works of Balzac. These works, it seems to me, constitute a novel form of their own, one that integrates important elements belonging to the two types of novels that I have mentioned and probably represents the most important form of fictional expression in history.'

The remarks formulated in these pages are an attempt to develop in greater detail the hypothesis hinted at in these lines.

2 Introduction to a Structural Study of Malraux's Novels

In order to determine the limits of this work, I should perhaps say at the outset that it makes no claim to being a completed sociological study of Malraux's literary writings.

Such a study, indeed, would presuppose, on the one hand, the elucidation of a number of significant structures capable of accounting, in large part at least, for the content and formal character of these writings and, on the other hand, a demonstration either of the homology or of the possibility of finding a significant relation between the structures of this literary world and a number of other social, economic, political, religious structures, etc.

My research is still situated at the first stage, that of internal analysis, and is intended as a rough sketch of the significant structures *immanent in the work*, a sketch that will very probably be altered and filled out by later research into the homologies and significant relations with the intellectual, social, political, or economic structures of the period in which they were elaborated.

As such, however, it seemed to me that, even at this provisional stage, the results of this study, hypothetical though they may be, are of sufficient interest to warrant publication.

In studying Malraux's work, one fact strikes one at the outset: between his earliest writings (*Le Royaume farfelu, Lunes en Papier, La Tentation de l'Occident*), which affirm the death of the Gods and the universal decline of values, and the following works (*Les Conquérants, La Voie royale, La Condition humaine*), there is not only a difference of content but also a difference of *form*. Although, in each case, we are dealing with works of fiction, only those of the second group create an avowedly realistic world made up of characters who, though imaginary, are both individual and alive, and therefore belong recognizably to the world of the novel, whereas those of the first are either, like *La Tentation de l'Occident*, essays, or, like *Le Royaume farfelu* and *Lunes en Papier*, fantastic and allegorical stories (despite Malraux's declaration at the head of *Lunes en Papier* that 'there is no symbol in this book').

If, moreover, we go on to observe that all Malraux's later novels were to create worlds governed by positive and universal values, and that the first work to indicate a new crisis, *La Lutte avec l'Ange* was to be both the last and the least novel-like, the most intellectual of Malraux's fictional writings, it seems to me that we might be able to formulate an initial hypothesis: *in this oeuvre, dominated by the crisis of values that characterized Western Europe in the period in which it was written, the creation of novels in the strict sense of the term corresponds to the period in which the writer believed that he was able, against all comers, to safeguard the existence of certain authentic universal values.*

Indeed, even the titles of the work, *Lunes en Papier, Le Royaume farfelu* on the one hand, and, on the other, *Les Conquérants, La Voie royale, La Condition humaine, Le Temps du Mépris, L'Espoir*, show the difference of content that led to the formal transformations and made possible the strictly novel-writing period in the writer's *oeuvre*.

However, if we take the phrase *strictly novel-writing* in a narrow sense, the period covers only three works: *Les Conquérants, La Voie royale*, and *La Condition humaine*. Only these can really be regarded as novels in the strict sense — *Le Temps du Mépris* and *L'Espoir* are narratives orientated towards a lyrico-epic form and *Les Noyers de l'Altenburg* is a *structured* series of stories intended in the first place to pose a *conceptual* problem. So it must be made clear that in this study we will be using the term 'novel-writing period' in a less rigorous and broader sense so as to comprise the six avowedly realistic works which, in Malraux's *oeuvre*, describe a world of individual and living characters.

Following a concrete principle of all sociological and genetic research that sets out to analyse, as far as possible, the content and structure of a writer's works in their chronological order, we shall, before embarking on our study of the novels, spend some time, however brief, on the three earlier works. In the absence of any precise information as to their date of composition, I shall approach them in the order that seems to me most amenable to analysis.[1]

Le Royaume farfelu (subtitled *Histoire*) is made up of two parts, one of which, according to a note in the Skira edition, was written in 1920, the whole having been published for the first time in 1927.

The essential content of this work seems to me to be both a consciousness of the vanity and universal death of values and the romantic aspiration to an unknown and unknowable value. In the first part, this value is embodied in the Princess of China who appears in dream to the Prince of the country — a Princess he has never seen and who is virtually identical with the blue flower of the German romantics.

Yet, although this aspiration towards an unknown and unattainable value forms the over-all background of the work, it is referred to explicitly only twice in the course of the twenty pages that make up the work in the Skira edition; it is true that these two passages occur at two particularly significant places: the first at the end of the first part[2], the second at the end of the work.

The other nineteen pages of the text develop, on the other hand, the theme of the universal death of values.

This theme defines the very time of the first part; the characters *were once* alive and significant but are so no longer. The opening lines indicate this at once. Devils and holy places, popes and anti-popes, emperors and conquerors were once but are so no longer and the memory of their past greatness merely colours the vanity of a durable and eternal present:

> Take care, curly-haired devils: pale images are silently forming over the sea; *this hour is no longer yours.* See, see: facing the *tombs* of the holy places, the watchers are slowly winding up the clocks that measure eternity by *dead* sultans — popes and gilded anti-popes pursue one another through the *deserted* sewers of Rome; behind them demons with silky tails that were *once* emperors laugh silently — . . . — a king who *no longer loves* anything but music and tortures wanders the night, desolate, blowing into tall silver trumpets, leading on his dancing people . . . and here at the frontier of the two Indies, beneath trees with leaves that nestle tightly together like beasts, an abandoned conqueror *sleeps* in his black armour, surrounded by anxious monkeys . . .[3]

And even what still exists is defined by the consciousness of its future destruction and by the seeping away of life. In the city in which the travellers arrive, a merchant selling phoenixes burns one before their eyes:

> The animal was reborn at once from its ashes, but took advantage of the imprudent joy of the merchant *to fly away*, on *heavy, graceless wings*. Consternation. All faces looked up, everyone followed the bird with his eyes; in the silence, one could hear nothing but voices in the distance crying: '*City born of the sea, one day the fishes of darkness will invade your animal-shaped palaces . . .*'

The immortal dragons, which are so beautiful that the mere sight of them 'vanquishes the greatest sorrows, the sharpest griefs', may also 'be used as a barometers'; in great cauldrons priests are brewing innumerable little gods made of yellow copper. Shut up in a dark cell the narrator feels 'imbued with a great sadness, . . . exhausted . . ., joyless . . .' He sees 'abandoned mansions', etc. He is led before the Prince of the country, who listens to the reports of the messengers announcing a universal death, but he refuses to accept them because he dreams of the Princess of China:

'Prince, I went to Babylon the *deserted* . . . The city is *nothing but dust . . .*'

'Good, I will go further, much further. Do you know hell, hell with its sky filled with violet stars . . . and, in its depths, its solemn chants? . . .'

'There is no chanting, Prince . . .'

Another messenger has taken the Prince's daughter to the fish-eating Tsar; in his account, we meet one of the most important images in the text, an image that we shall find repeatedly in Malraux's early writings, and which seems to me to have had particular significance for him. The image is of the gods who once reigned hidden in temples or underground caves and who emerged in times of fire or invasion, only to become mere mechanical toys or to vanish entirely. In any case, they have lost all their powers:

'. . . Silent invasions are in preparation . . . The Princess, surrounded by white tom cats, ordered all the gods of the conquered peoples to be brought before her, in a cellar full of millepedes, and chained them one to another . . . One day, the temple burst into flames: the blackened idols emerged from the flames, the Tsar's guards fought with blue axes against the whirlwinds of rebellious horsemen who brandished the oiled skulls of huge animals . . .'

'And now?'

'Now, the tsarina reigns alone. With the thaw, the last idols descended the river like heavy boats (there is a great cemetery for them at the river's mouth . . .). From the palace the tsarina showed their dead fleet to the imprisoned gods of the tributaries, to the bound, mildewed gods that she had had chained to the bars of the window, as the Christian priests continued with their chanting.'

The second part of the work recounts the expedition and defeat of an army that did not go into battle, having met with no resistance, but only an abandoned city, transformed into a labyrinth and inhabited by birds, lizards, and, finally, scorpions. It is the story of an army that has become bogged down — to the point of becoming a victim of scorpions (for it no longer has the energy to defend itself) — in the soft mass of a reality that is devoid of structure because it has lost all values.

It is a recapitulation of the first part in a narrative mode. We should note as particularly significant the reappearance of the image of the gods emerging from underground who lose all their powers when exposed to the light of day.[4] We should also note the epilogue in which the narrator, a survivor from the massacre, is a prematurely aged man, leading a life devoid of all interest and living with the memory of defeat. This epilogue ends the story with a romantic image similar to that of the Princess of China with which the first part ended: 'Perhaps I will take one of those ships that set sail for the Islands of the Blest. I have scarcely reached my sixtieth year . . .'

Of course, this piece, written by a young man of twenty or twenty-seven who already feels old, and for whom values are no more than a memory, is not a work of great literary value.

A critic who had only this text to go on would probably see in it the superficial and perhaps verbal disenchantment of a very gifted, but excessively self-centred adolescent.

What came after the work, however, shows us that it was something quite different. It possesses, among other things, an acute sensitivity to the intellectual and moral crisis of the Western world, as felt by one of the most restless and most powerful intellects of the period. Above all, of course, it provides the foundation for his future work, and as such it required, it seemed to me, a few pages of analysis. For the same reason, I shall deal very briefly with the content of the two following works.

A similar vision is to be found in *Lunes en Papier,* which appeared for the first time in 1920.

The work is connected explicitly with *Le Royaume farfelu* since we are told that the kingdom in question is also death's empire.[5]

It, too, is composed of two parts: a five-page prologue, in the Skira edition, and a twenty-two page narrative, which, as in *Le Royaume farfelu,* takes up a similar theme from the first part.

The influence of avant-garde literature is obvious enough, not only in the form, but also in the content; the piece relates in effect the struggles of nonconformist writers against the *Royaume Farfelu,*[6] the Empire of Death, the bourgeois society of the period.[7] However, Malraux does not believe in this struggle, and it is the vanity of such a struggle that he recounts twice in a symbolic and even allergorical mode.

In the prologue, the universe consists of a moonlit lake ruled over by a genie in the form of a cat. The teeth of this genie come out and flit about over the water where they meet the balloons that are attacking the genie and the castle formed by the reflection of the moonlight in the water. The context makes it clear that these balloons are writers, while the moon-children, the castle, and the genie of the lake are symbols of society as a whole.

The moon-children believe above all that writers are nonconformist characters, mysterious perhaps, but serious and important. Once this illusion has been dissipated, conflict breaks out. Having met the balloons:

the moon-children, young as they were, believed that they were
working at invisible and complicated works. With the knowledge of
the truth, they were overcome with indignation: their noses turned
into billiard cues and projected the aerostats over the lake. Though
plump, they were light and rebounded; and their harmonious
elegance aroused the jealousy of the moons who wanted their death.

This wish was not granted. Since they would no longer idle away
their time, the balloons, alas!, were forced to act! . . .

Having seen the castle outlined by the reflection of the moon on the
lake, they decided to invade it:

To this end, one of them stepped forward and began to read a
didactic play he had written when still at school. The contemptuous
palace did not reply. Such disdain proved fatal! The aerostats
continued to read. By the time he reached the word 'Curtain', the
palace had fallen into a deep sleep. All the balloons leapt up, one
appearing like a cockade, in the frame of each window. They entered
without difficulty.

In the conquered castle they find 'Punches, policemen, game-
keepers, brides, devils, countrymen with red umbrellas, concierges, and
nonentities of all kinds.'

They tie them up and bind them to the windows in order to project
on to them their own children and horseradishes full of sound who are
philosophers. The phantoms fall with a click.

However, before this rout, the genie of the lake goes into the attack.
He brings up a barrel that fills the balloons with terror; they are afraid
it contains an explosive; however, the bravest among them go up to it;
the barrel contains something much more dangerous than an explosive:
very old brandy. The balloons get drunk, and the genie of the lake is
able to tie them up. Victorious, he cries:

Look at these fine balloons, they are my prisoners, I am not selling
them, I am giving them away, doesn't anyone want one? . . . Well,
since nobody wants the balloons, we, the Genie of this lake . . .
condemn them to death . . . They will be hanged.

He tries to attach the balloons to an inflation-tube to hang them and
make them put out their tongues, but they resist:

Their tongues persist in playing hide and seek! They persist!

They persist. My life has irremediably failed. O passion, you will
lose your plaything! . . .

And the genie of the lake:

> hanged himself at the end of his beads, his paws crossed, as was only fitting.
> Then, as his weight had increased, the beads stretched; each bead stuck out its tongue; and the charm, which was a cat with crossed paws, stuck out a victorious tongue that seemed to be pretending to strike the others but fell back, limp, as if it had been burst with a pin.

This summary has no need of commentary. The work is obviously a satire on nonconformist writers and thinkers who set out to do battle against the society of nonentities who occupy the castle, corrupted by a barrel of brandy, and sinking at the end into the universal death that invades the universe.

The second part, divided into three chapters, *Combats, Voyages, Victoire*, recounts the struggles of these same nonconformist intellectuals (who assume here the form of the seven deadly sins walking on their hands;[8] five of them were born directly from a fruit that itself issued from the transformation of one of the balloons and the other two proceed from the replacement of the two dead characters by a scientist and a musician) against death and its '*royaume farfelu*'.

It is, of course, useless to insist on the different, and generally symbolic, episodes that mark this journey and this battle; let us merely remember the fact that in order to fight the seven deadly sins death sends two extremely dangerous weapons, the telephone serpents and the geissler tubes, which the deadly sins will combat with the help of a phonograph and an electricity capsule. This means that the two most powerful weapons of the Empire of Death against writers and thinkers are the pseudo-culture of the 'mass media' and industrial technology, but also that in order to combat them writers employ weapons that are essentially related to them, which makes their struggle questionable and ambiguous. The end of the work throws some light on Malraux's position. Death has, in effect, become modernized, or more exactly industrialized. It has aluminium vertebrae and brass joints. Disguised as a doctor, Pride prescribes for her a bath of nitric acid in which she will be corroded and destroyed. Only when the victory of the sins appears finally assured, Malraux ends his work in the following way:

> Death was dead. Seated on the highest battlements of the castle tower, the sins watched the evening caress the calm city. No change appeared yet.
> 'And now to work!' said Pride.

'To work!!' repeated the sins.

'Where shall we begin?' asked Hifili.

There was a long silence, which was ended when, after some hesitation, the musician said:

'Excuse me, dear friends . . . When I was a man, I was subject to mental anaemia . . . Don't therefore be surprised at my question: Why have we killed Death?'

The sins had hung bits of her skeleton from their belts as memory joggers . . .

'Yes, why have we killed Death?'

They looked at one another. Their faces were sad. They then held their heads in their hands and wept. Why had they killed Death? They had all forgotten.

The end is thus at the same time different from the first part and similar to it. The first time the world had defeated the writers, the second time it is the writers who are victorious, but in either case the victory is deprived of meaning, for victors and vanquished sink into the same universal death.

The same ideas are taken up again on a conceptual level in the work constituted by an exchange of letters between an Oriental intellectual travelling in Europe and a Western intellectual living in China — *La Tentation de l'Occident.*

The title suggests the temptation represented for the West by the rest of the world and, in particular, the East, since its own values have lost their vitality and are in the grip of a fatal disease. But even if, in an explicit way, the title and most of the work concern the crisis of Western culture, the last letters indicate that Chinese culture is undergoing no less a crisis of a complementary kind with similar consequences. Just as the West falls back on foreign customs that it understands without actually liking, so young Chinese feel drawn by the Western culture they hate. In either case this attitude is due to the decline, in each of these civilizations, of specific values (individualism in the West, a pantheism of the sensibility in the East) and of the barriers that the vitality of these values once opposed to the appeals and attraction of alien cultures.

So as not to stretch the scope of this study too far, I will content myself with mentioning two passages that seem to me to be particularly significant.

In the first place, in order to denote the crisis in Chinese culture, there is the reappearance of the image of the great fire that has destroyed all values:

... I would like the date of our national festival to be no longer the anniversary of our sick children's revolution, but of that evening when the intelligent soldiers of the allied armies fled from the Summer Palace, carefully carrying with them the precious mechanical toys that ten centuries had given the Emperor, crushing the pearls and wiping their boots on the courtly capes of tributary kings ...

The word 'gods' is missing in this passage — which, indeed, is perfectly analogous with the two passages already quoted from *Le Royaume farfelu* and with the one we shall meet later in *Les Conquérants* — for the simple reason that Malraux, in the mouth of the old Chinese thinker Wang-Loh, had just defined the old Chinese culture as a culture without gods. Of the present crisis he says: '. . . It is the destruction, the crushing of the greatest of the human systems, of a system that succeeded in living without depending either on the gods or on men. The crushing of it! . . .'

The second passage is the description of the crisis in Western culture. The disappearance of the transcendent values of the Middle Ages resulted — and here Malraux's penetration is remarkable — in the crisis of individualistic values which, in classical culture, had replaced the divinity, and the impossibility of creating new structures or forms that could no longer be based either on the trans-individual or on the individual:

... Absolute reality for you has been first God, then man; but, *after God, man has died and you seek anxiously for the one to whom you might entrust this strange inheritance.* Your paltry attempts at structure for modest nihilisms do not look as if they will last for long ...

But, and this assumes a particular interest in the light of Malraux's latest writings on art and is of interest here because it illustrates the extent to which the same facts may have opposite significations and values when integrated into different mental structures, Malraux designates as symptomatic of the crisis and decline of Western culture the appearance of the Imaginary Museum, which, a few decades later, was to be seen by him as the most secure foundation of this culture and even of the human condition:

... *The Europeans are tired of themselves, tired of their disintegrating individualism*, tired of their exaltation. What sustains them is not so much an ideology as a delicate structure of negations. Capable of acting to the point of sacrifice, *but filled with disgust when*

confronted with the will to action that twists their race today, they
would like to seek beneath the acts of men *a deeper reason for
being. One by one, their defences are disappearing.* They do not wish
to oppose what is offered to their sensibility, they can no longer not
understand. It is when they consider works of art that the tendency
that drives them to abandon themselves dominates them most. Art,
then, is a pretext, and the most delicate of pretexts: the subtlest of
temptations, it is the temptation that we know is reserved for the
best. *There is no imaginary world that the restless European artists
of today are not striving to conquer. An abandoned palace attacked
by the winter wind, our mind is disintegrating little by little, and its
highly decorative cracks are growing ever wider . . .* These works, and
the pleasure they bring, cannot be 'learnt' like a foreign language;
but hidden by their succession, *one can guess at a terrifying force
that dominates the mind.* There is, in this search ever to renew certain
aspects of the world by looking at them with new eyes, an eager
ingenuity that acts on man in a stupefying way. The dreams that
have possessed us call forth other dreams, however their spell is
worked: plant, picture or book. *The special pleasure one finds in
discovering unknown arts ceases with their discovery and is not
turned into love.* Let other forms come that will move us, and that
we will not love, *sick kings to whom each day brings the finest
presents of the kingdom, to whom each evening brings a faithful and
desperate avidity . . . . It is the world that is invading Europe,
the world with all its present and all its past,* its piled-up offerings of
living or dead forms and meditations . . . This great troubled
spectacle that is beginning, my dear friend, is *one of the temptations
of the West.*

The profound crisis of Western civilization, the crisis of individualistic values and of the hopes that buttress them up, is expressed among
other things in a crisis of action and also, as we have seen, in a crisis of
love, a general crisis of values in which only one attitude survives —
knowledge:

A declining reality seeks the support of myths, and prefers those
that are born of the mind. What is called up by the vision of
intangible forces, slowly re-erecting the old effigy of fatality, in our
civilization whose magnificent, and perhaps fatal, law is that *any
temptation can be resolved in knowledge? . . .* There is at the heart
of the Western world *a hopeless conflict,* in whatever form we find
it: *it is the conflict between man and what he has created.*

So the book ends on a refusal of the narcotic offered by Christianity:

> '. . . the higher faith: that offered by every village cross and the same crosses that stand over our dead.'
> '. . . I will never accept it; I will not lower myself before it to ask for the peace that my weakness craves . . .'

and on a clear, desperate act of awareness which, at this period, is Malraux's last word:

> Eager Lucidity, I still burn before thee, solitary and upright flame, in this heavy night in which the yellow wind howls, as in all those alien nights when the ocean wind repeated around me the proud clamour of the sterile sea . . .

Between *Le Royaume farfelu, Lunes en Papier, Le Tentation de l'Occident*, on the one hand, and *Les Conquérants*, on the other, there is a qualitative leap: the transformation of a young man who writes in a remarkable way, but whose fiction is neither original nor profound, into one of the greatest writers of the first half of the twentieth century in Western Europe. This transformation no doubt involved progress in the technique of writing and in mastery of style; but had it been due only to this progress, it would have appeared gradually and certainly could not have accounted for the transformation that occurs, on the contrary, as a *sudden, qualitative* change.

Two other arguments can be used to support this case: on the one hand, the long-held opinion of sociologists of culture, which is invariably confirmed by concrete research, that qualitative changes within an *oeuvre*, a style, a literary or artistic genre, are always born, even when they involve important technical changes, from a new content that finally creates its own means of expression; and, on the other hand, the later evolution of Malraux himself, who, from 1939, a period of which he was certainly to the highest degree master of his writing and of his style, nevertheless ceased writing literary works and returned, no doubt at a much higher level, to essays and conceptual works.

Would it be too daring to remind ourselves here of our initial hypothesis that the *properly literary* work of the writer, the possibility of his creating concrete imaginary worlds in a realistic way, was closely bound up with a faith in human values that were universally accessible to all men, the conceptual writings corresponding on the contrary to the *absence* of such a faith, that this absence took the form either of the earlier disillusion or of the theory of creative élites that appears first in *Les Noyers de l'Altenburg* and is developed from *Le Musée imaginaire* onwards.

Between *Les Conquérants* and *La Condition humaine*, Malraux the novelist is a man who *believes* in *universal if problematic values*. The Malraux of *Le Temps du Mépris* and *L'Espoir* is a man who believes in universal, *transparent*, but highly *threatened* values. The author of *Les Noyers de l'Altenburg*, a work midway between literary creation and conceptual reflection, is a man who recounts his disillusion and is still seeking a basis for his faith in man.

Subsequently, there is the essayist and art historian who lies outside this study, for what we are concerned with here is Malraux the writer and his vision, or more exactly his visions and their literary expressions.

We do not know in what order *Les Conquérants* and *La Voie royale* were written. Although important, it is not a decisive question, for the two books have a similar structure and complement one another. Furthermore, they immediately place Malraux among the great writers of the twentieth century, because they bring a new and original solution to the most important problem which, in different and complementary forms, was preoccupying Western philosophy at the time: what significance can be given to the inner life in a general crisis of values.

Let us try at the very relative level of a research that is still in its beginnings to sketch this situation both in literature and in philosophy.

In my studies on the sociology of the novel I have characterized this period as one of *transition* between two novel forms that were in intelligible relation with the whole of the social and economic structure. The first of these, that of the novel with a problematic hero, corresponded to the liberal economy and was bound up with the value, universally recognized and grounded in reality, of every individual life as such. The second form, the novel of a non-biographical character, corresponded to societies in which the liberal market, and, with it, individualism had already been superseded.

Now, if the novel with a problematic hero and the non-biographical novel constitute relatively unitary and stable structures, there lies between them a *period of transition*, much more varied and richer in types of fictional creation, born of the fact that, on the one hand, the disappearance of the economic and social foundation of individualism meant that writers could no longer content themselves with the problematic character *as such* without relating him to a reality that was exterior to him and, on the other, economic, social, and cultural evolution is not yet sufficiently advanced to create the conditions for a definitive crystallization of the novel\without hero and without character.

It must not be imagined, of course, that these three periods are clearly marked off in time. Social life is a complex reality and its different aspects are superimposed one upon another; a few writers were already developing novels without characters, others were still at the stage of a novel with a problematic hero, while others again were in what I have called the period of transition. The distinction of three successive periods, was, in the first place, a schematization intended as a framework for research.[9]

In any case, Malraux's first novels are situated in the general line of the novel of transition, whose problematic is that of the subject and the meaning of action and, as much as possible, of *individual* action in a world where the individual no longer represents value simply by virtue of being an individual. And the importance of *Les Conquérants* and *La Voie royale* resides in the fact that, having integrated at a very advanced level the consciousness of the problem of the crisis of values already expressed in a radical way in his first three works, Malraux nevertheless presents a solution on the *individual* biographical level while many other writers (including himself from *La Condition humaine* onwards) are orientated towards replacing the individual hero with a *collective* character.

In short, *Les Conquérants* and *La Voie royale* are among the last great attempts to write a novel *with a problematic hero*, while remaining fully aware of the fact that the life of heroes of this type can no longer be enough and that, in order to give it meaning, it must be superseded in the direction of a certain social and historical context. Let us say at the outset, before we even begin a structural description of the two works, that, from this point of view, the heroes must necessarily be *men of action*.

Don Quixote, Julien Sorel, Emma Bovary were interesting by virtue of their own psychology; Garine and Perken cannot be separated from their action. This is not an incidental detail or the expression of a psychological preference on the part of Malraux, but a structural necessity of their characters.

Without their efforts to achieve certain ends *in the external world*, without the *seriousness* of this effort (and this seriousness is expressed in the fact that it can be carried quite naturally to the assumption of the possibility of suicide and the *risk of death*), their characters would be entirely devoid of interest. Malraux's heroes, and particularly Garine and Perken, have often been accused of being adventurers. Malraux himself has tried to disprove this charge by contrasting, for example, Perken with Mayrena, or Claude with his father.

The terminology does not of course interest me and I am quite unconcerned as to what might be meant by an 'adventurer', but the distinction made by Malraux seems to me to be important for an understanding of his work. Mayrena and Claude's grandfather are interested directly in themselves, in the style of their action and life. Garine, Perken, and even Claude are exclusively interested in the ends that they pursue, their *action* is *serious* because it is orientated above all towards victory and their life-styles result precisely from the fact that they do not think of style while acting.

Before continuing with the analysis, I should say something about the intellectual context in which Malraux's reply was made, about the way in which the problem of values in conceptual thinking in general and philosophical thinking in particular was presented in this critical period of Western consciousness.

Indeed, from another angle, the crisis of individualism had brought the same problems of action and death to the centre of the philosophical problematic.[10]

In the Christian ideology of the Middle Ages, death was for the individual a particularly important problem, for it marked the balance-sheet of his life, the moment at which was to be decided, *once and for all*, the character of his eternal existence, the fact that he would be eternally rejected or saved. Nevertheless, it was not the essential problem since it was subordinated to that of salvation.

Later, however, when the individual *qua* individual had become a universal value, he was no longer, or at least to a diminishing degree, to encounter the problem at which he would no longer exist; the individualistic values of reason and experience remain eternal in so far as there will always be individuals who really pursue them or are able to pursue them. As long as the individual exists he is of value *qua* individual; as soon as he is dead, he no longer exists either as a value or as a problem; that is why, as I have said elsewhere, individualistic philosophies are potentially amoral, unaesthetic[11], and areligious in their tendencies.

In the twentieth century the crisis of individualistic values which, as we have already seen, emerged from the suppression of the liberal market and resulted, in literature, in the decline of the traditional novel with a problematic hero, not only reintroduced, at the level of conceptual thought, the problem of death, but even placed it at the centre of the philosophical problematic.

If the behaviour of the individual can no longer be based either on trans-individual values (since individualism had suppressed them all) or on the unchallengeable value of the individual (now open to question), thought had necessarily to be centred on the difficulties of this grounding, on the limits of the human being *qua* individual and on the most important of those limitations, his inevitable disappearance, death.

The Pascalian position was thus reintroduced, but it is certainly no accident that about 1910 it was re-expressed for the first time in a great philosophical work: Georg Lukács's *The Metaphysics of Tragedy*. The problem that absorbed the philosophers of the period in the most acute and consious manner was indeed that of the absence of any grounding for values and the absence of any possibilities for surmounting that absence; in this situation, individual behaviour presented itself under two complementary aspects. It could be related to the individual as essentially limited by death and coming into conflict with death in his effort to find a meaning (all individual meaning being necessarily reduced to nothingness by the death of the individual who grounded it), or it could be related to society and the community of men, as an *absence* of any form of trans-individual reality and therefore as the difficulty of finding in external action a full, valid meaning. In short, deprived of two possible groundings, *the individual* and *trans-individual realities*, human behaviour found itself put in question and this crisis assumed for philosophical thought the form of the double problem of *death* and *action*.

It is to this problematic that Malraux's first two novels constitute a coherent and powerfully original reply.

At the time at which *Les Conquérants* appeared, Lukács had already made two contradictory replies to this question. In 1908 in *The Metaphysics of Tragedy*, he had declared that the absolute reality of death as limit and the absence of all trans-individual reality rendered impossible *in the world* any authentic life, any valid action, since authenticity could no longer be situated for him in the clear consciousness of this limit and in the grandeur of a radical and intended refusal.

In 1923, having become a Marxist, he affirmed the reality of a trans-individual subject of history: the revolutionary proletariat and, therefore, the possibility of meaningful life and action, and the secondary character, in the final analysis, of death, which was no more than an individual fact incapable of affecting the true subject of thought and action.

However different these two positions may be, the reader will no doubt notice that they have an element in common: the reciprocal exclusion of meaningful action and death as fundamental human realities. In 1908, the essential reality of death supresses for Lukács any possibility of meaningful action; in 1923 the possibility of action relegates inversely the problem of death to a secondary level.

On this point, Heidegger's thinking as expressed in *Sein und Zeit* is essentially different, though it is working with the same elements. In the final analysis it is the synthesis that preserves both Lukács's positions, a synthesis culminating in the affirmation of the possibility of co-existence between authenticity, an acute consciousness of the reality of death, and a certain mode of meaningful action in the world.

Like Lukács in 1908, Heidegger thinks in 1927 that the only possibility of an authentic existence is that of life for and towards death (*Sein zum Tode*). However, like Lukács in 1923, Heidegger thinks that this authentic individual existence may be realized in historical action, not by virtue of the reality of a trans-individual collective subject, but by the repetition (authentic and non-mechanical) of the attitude and behaviour of the great figures of the nation's past.

The grounding in Heidegger's philosophy of this survival of values at the death of the individual is a particularly difficult philosophical problem. Perhaps it implies the underlying idea of an authentic community not of men as such but of individuals constituting a creative élite. If this interpretation were valid, it would, in fact, be a position fairly close to the one Malraux was to develop in his writings on art. However, this problem does not concern us at the moment. Suffice it to say that for any writer or thinker who is still seeking an individualistic vision of universal scope, Lukács's position in 1908 presented the difficulty of denying any possibility of authentic life in the world, that of 1923 the difficulty of denying the primordial character of the individual, and that of Heidegger in *Sein und Zeit* the difficulty of reconciling the essential importance of death for every authentic individual consciousness with the survival of the value of projects and individual actions beyond the disappearance of the individual.

In the present state of my research I still know nothing of the biographical and historical genesis of Malraux's ideas; but the vision that underlies *Les Conquérants* and *La Voie royale* and enables Malraux to create a particular form of novel with a problematic hero is, quite obviously, situated in the intellectual context that I have just described. For in these novels death and meaningful action no doubt exclude one another as presences, but may nevertheless constitute a structure in so far as they succeed one another in time.

While ever the individual is alive, the authenticity of his life resides in his total commitment to the revolutionary action of liberation, with an exclusive concern for victory, and this action relegates death to a place that is no doubt real, but nevertheless secondary. It exists for the hero only as an ever-present limit, whose incorporation in consciousness alone renders his action serious.

But it also constitutes a potential and inevitable reality alien to action, whose re-activation must necessarily, and *retroactively*, deprive of value any action that found its grounding only in the individual.

While ever Garine or Perken acts, death exists for them only as a risk and limit of action, the assumption of which lends seriousness and validity to this action. With the approach of death, their action *retroactively* loses all value and they find themselves alone once again like Pascal's man or Lukács's man in *The Metaphysics of Tragedy.*

As for the structure constituted by this synthesis of action and death, it creates an individual *sui generis* who is neither the tragic man of Pascal and the first Lukács, nor the romantic genius of Heidegger, but Garine and Perken, the nonconformists, revolutionary, *problematic* and *sick* men of action of Malraux's first two novels.

It is from this point of view that I shall now analyse Malraux's next two works – as I have already said, we do not know which of the two was written first.

Les Conquérants, which appeared in 1927, is composed of three parts whose titles sum up the novel: *Outward Bound, The Powers, The Man.*

The story itself is recounted by a young man who leaves Europe to arrive at the place where he will meet the hero of the novel and where a decisive episode in historical development will take place.

From the first line, however, Malraux indicates that Garine does not exist in an autonomous manner, in himself. In the over-all plan, *the man* arrives only after *the powers*; and the voyage is not simply that which leads the narrator toward Garine, it is above all a voyage to the place that enables Garine to have a meaningful existence, to be himself; the novel opens by stating in the same sentence both the place of the action and its nature, the essence of the universe that it describes: 'A general strike has been declared at Canton.'[1 2]

It is not merely an incident, extremely important perhaps but nevertheless of the same nature as many others. It is, in the novel, a radical transformation of the world, the moment at which this world begins to exist and at which life becomes finally possible. In the passive, decomposing world that Malraux had described in his previous works, something appears that brings back life and constitutes a new value: action and more specifically revolutionary historical action.

In this world with which he is not identified (he is neither Chinese nor a professional revolutionary and that is why he can be the hero of the novel), Garine will be able to become an essential character and — what amounts to the same thing — give meaning and value to his existence.

If we place ourselves at a very general level, we could content ourselves with saying that Malraux discovered in historical action the possibility of original literary creation. This might be enough for a phenomenological study. As a sociologist, I would also have to state that this action has in Malraux's fictional *oeuvre* a concrete form, determined by the period, that of his encounter with the communist world and ideology; we should therefore pause briefly and examine this encounter.

Although I have not yet embarked on an examination in depth of even the most important works of fiction written between the two Wars, it seems to me that Malraux is the only writer, apart from Victor Serge, to make the proletarian revolution an important structural element in his novels. Indeed, between 1927 and 1939, Malraux was the only great novelist of this revolution in France. This is a measure of the importance for him of the encounter that enabled him to create a true fictional world, the encounter with the communist ideology which quite obviously appeared to him first as the only authentic reality in a declining world.

Quite obviously, too, Malraux was not a communist, either in his earliest novels, *Les Conquérants, La Voie royale*, and *La Condition humaine*, nor in his last truly literary work, *Les Noyers de l'Altenburg*. The works written from a point of view closest to official communist thinking was *Le Temps du Mépris* and, above all, *L'Espoir*. This observation presents anyone who seeks to undertake a sociological study of Malraux's writing with at least two groups of important problems. The first, which presupposes an enormous amount of empirical research, concerns the questions as to what extent Malraux's fairly complex relations with communist ideology between 1925 and 1933 is an individual phenomenon or, on the contrary, expresses a more general fact resulting from the meeting of preoccupations that dominated certain groups of French intellectuals with the reality of the Russian revolution and the world revolutionary movement; the second, of a strictly aesthetic order, concerns the relation between the place occupied in this vision by the communist movement and the literary form of the works themselves.

Indeed, it is no accident that the novel form of the three first works (*Les Conquérants, La Voie royale, La Voie royale, La Condition humaine*) coincides with a complex relation that implies both a community and a distance between the writer and the movement, whereas in *Le Temps du Mépris* and *Le Espoir*, when the proximity becomes more important than the distance, we see this strictly novel form burst open to reveal a new literary form *sui generis* that still remains to be analysed. Let me say finally that *Les Noyers de l'Altenburg*, an intermediary work from the formal point of view between literary creation and the essay, can also be defined to a large degree by the relation between Malraux and communism, in so far as one of the aspects of this work concerns the radical break with communism.

Before embarking on an analysis of *Les Conquérants*, let me also say that there are two important texts concerning this novel that seem to me to be based on a single misunderstanding. These are a letter by Trotsky that deals with the book as if it were a political tract, completely ignoring its literary character and the formal requirements of the novel structure, and, curiously enough, an epilogue added by Malraux for the republication of the novel in the Pléiade series, in which he explains why he rejected communism, and in which he places himself, no doubt from an opposed point of view, on the same level as Trotsky's letter. It goes without saying that in my analysis I shall try on the contrary to remain on the level of the study of an imaginary world – grounded no doubt in the social and political reality of the period and for the study of which the political convictions of the writer constitute one of the explanatory factors, but only one among others, and not always the most important (for the sociologist of literature knows that very often formal requirements predominate over the conceptual convictions of the author) a world that nevertheless has its own structural requirements that must be understood and elucidated:

A general strike has been declared at Canton.

For the life of the Chinese coolies and for Chinese civilization in general this fact indicates a decisive turning-point:

You know how innocent China used to be of any ideas tending to action. Now they have taken possession of her much as the idea of equality took possession of the French in '89 . . . Now at Canton, things were not so simple, but no less terrible. Of no kind of individualism had they the remotest idea. Today coolies are beginning to discover that they exist, simply that they exist . . . Nationalist propaganda, as carried on by Garine, told them something quite different; it moved them, in a way quite unforeseen and extraordinarily violent, by teaching them to believe in their own dignity . . . The strength of the French revolution and the Russian revolution, lay in the fact that they gave everyone his land. This revolution is giving everyone his life . . . This Borodin has not yet understood . . . (1956:16–17)

The last few phrases show at once that in the novel the Chinese revolution assumes a particular and different importance from that of the Russian revolution and international communism. Indeed, the text itself marks this distinction: 'This Borodin has not yet understood . . .' (1956:17)

Other passages indicate the same thing; the narrator, on his way to Canton, reads the messages and reacts according to the importance that the various places and things have in the world of the novel:

England, Belgium, the United States, nothing of importance there – but what next? Russia? Ah! No, nothing worth noting. China. At last!
The President of the Republic.
What then?
Canton! (1956:2)[1][3]

In this passage, the names of countries and cities are not mere geographical or sociological observations but the description of the structure of the fictional space.

Canton and China in the centre, Russia further away, England, Belgium, etc., outside its frontiers and therefore indifferent.

Now Malraux, and of course most of the critics felt this, remains a Western writer concerned with the problems of the West. If, in order to write novels of the revolution, he situates their action in China and Spain, it is because the revolutionary movements occur there and because, when writing a work of realistic ambitions, he must situate its action as close as possible to reality. It seems to me however that, in these novels and perhaps in the thinking of most left-wing intellectuals of the time, one can find *no trace* of any awareness of a fact that has become obvious for us today: namely, that China in particular and the non-industrialized countries in general have their own problems, different from those that arise in Western societies, and that different evolutions are taking place in both groups of countries.

When speaking of China, Malraux wishes neither to take refuge in exoticism nor to describe a particular situation. He speaks instead of universal man and, implicitly, of Western man, of himself, and of his comrades.

From this point of view, China, Canton, the struggle against Britain represent the historical, universal, revolutionary action, the liberating action that brings to man a new awareness of his existence and his dignity. And, of course, the world of the novel is organized entirely on the axis of this action: foreign capitalism, represented particularly by Britain, with her allies in China itself, embodies the antagonistic powers, and, significantly, Soviet Russia, with its representatives in the novel, Klein, Borodin, Nikolaieff, constitute a positive allied force, but nevertheless one that is alien to and different from the Chinese revolution.

The first part, *Outward Bound*, recounts how the traveller sees the world of the novel gradually emerge in the course of his voyage. We know already that this world is made up of elements indicated by the titles of the two other parts of the book: *The Powers* (the Chinese revolution supported by Russia and the communists, and, on the opposite side, Britain) and *The Man* (Garine).

Within the over-all framework formed by the conflicting powers, let us examine the internal structure of the revolutionary power and the principal characters that embody it. There are first of all the Chinese masses, described in their complex structuration, from the poor people of Indo-China, passive sympathizers content to support the revolution with their financial aid, to the union cadres and Military School students. I shall not spend much time in analysing them. To do so would go well beyond the bounds envisaged for this study, important as this problem no doubt is. These masses form the background of the work.

As for the individuals, there are, in the foreground, Garine and Borodin, 'the two great idols'.

At first sight, one might be tempted to describe them as 'Malraux's hero and the communist militant', but this would be an extreme simplification for, in the novel, communism is represented by three characters who quite obviously embody, from the point of view of Garine and Malraux himself, three constitutive and distinct elements of the communist movement, each possessing a different human value: Klein, Borodin, and Nikolaieff.

The first, Klein, is the devoted militant, with no reservations, closely linked to the people (in the novel this link is expressed through his relationship with his wife, an integral embodiment of the oppressed people) who devotes his entire life to the Party and whose action will lead to torture and death.

Borodin is the revolutionary leader, the man of action for whom, however, action can exist only as a *struggle against oppression.* I should say at once that as Garine's action is structured and threatened by the boundary of death, that of Borodin is structured and threatened by a different boundary, but one with a similar function, that of victory; as a professional revolutionary, Borodin could never become a ruler or a statesman. That is why in the novel, where illness is the expression of an action whose future threatens to destroy its meaning retroactively, he is like Garine, though for different reasons, *seriously ill*.

Lastly, Nikolaieff, the eternal policeman, as he was under tsarism, as he now is in China, as he will always be, for whom victory can bring no change; limited, tough, however, and carrying out useful functions, but scarcely possessing a human value.

In this novel of the revolution Garine and Borodin are 'the two great idols' because their life is closely linked to the revolutionary action itself and cannot be conceived apart from it; their existence will lose all meaning as soon as this action stops, for Garine through death, for Borodin through the victory of the party to which he belongs.

Around them, the two most important characters, Hong and Chen-Dai, embody the abstract, principled attitude, unconnected with the concrete situation and the consequences of their acts. Hong, the anarchist, on the material plane of the action; Chen-Dai, on the spiritual, abstract plane of principles. Hong arrives at the stage of wishing to kill at all cost the rich and the powerful; Chen-Dai is opposed on principle to all violence. At bottom, they are both, each in his own way, Kantian moralists and idealists.

Thus, having encountered during his voyage the powers that constitute not the framework but the very elements of the novel structure, the narrator – and Malraux – are finally able by means of a police document to introduce, moving from the external to the essential, the central character of the novel: Garine.

The document first states 'militant anarchist', but the narrator, who once knew him, corrects this description: although he had frequented anarchist circles, he had never been an anarchist himself. What preoccupied him was not a particular ideal, but how meaning could be given to his life:

> In 1914, at twenty, he had just completed his course in literature and was deeply impressed by the great conflicting forces in life. Are any books besides memoirs worth writing? Systems were nothing to him. He was ready to adopt any that cicumstances might impose on him. (1956:52)

A little later, when speaking of the anarchists, he says: 'Those fools want to prove themselves in the right. But in practice there is only one "right", which is not a parody, and that is the efficient use of force.' (1956:52)

And this use can exist only when committed to the struggle for a precise end and not turned towards oneself:

'It is not so much the soul of a man that makes a leader,' he said to me one day, 'but his achievements.' 'Unfortunately', he added ironically. And, a few days later – he was reading *Le Mémorial* – 'It is achievement more than anything that sustains a leader's soul. Napoleon at St Helena actually said: "What a romance my life has been all the same!" Thus even genius rots!' (1956:53)

Having been implicated in some obscure business concerning financial aid to young women seeking abortion, he finds himself one day, in Geneva, under a police charge and about to be brought before a court. The only feeling that the trial arouses in him is of the total absurdity of the comedy being enacted before him and of his participation, even externally, in a society in which he discovers himself to be totally alien.

He then joins the Foreign Legion, where he finds war to be just as far removed from authentic action as anarchism and deserts before very long. In Zurich he comes into contact with Bolshevik *émigrés*. At first, he takes them to be mere theoreticians. Then, one day, he discovers to his astonishment that these doctrinaires had organized and carried through a revolution.

Having encountered revolutionary efficacy for the first time, he tries to make use of his connections in order to visit Russia. He does not succeed, but manages instead to get himself sent to China where he turns the propaganda office, which was entrusted to him more or less by chance, and which was not a very important institution, into one of the main centres of revolutionary action. It is through him and his organization that the transformation of China that paralyses the enemy in the strike at Canton becomes possible. I should add that in the course of his voyage the narrator happened to learn that this action which, seen from the outside, seemed so magnificent and so effective, was being undermined by innumerable internal dangers: lack of money, the power of the enemy, its agents in the Chinese camps, the immense authority of Chen-Dai, who is opposed to violence, etc.

The game, in fact, is far from being over. On the contrary, we are at the moment when it is about to be decided and victory or defeat will give meaning to the stake that Garine has placed on it: his life.

Lastly in this description of the functional character and his problematic, Malraux has kept until the last lines of the first part the end of the police document, the decisive element that defines Garine's structural status: 'I venture to lay special stress on the following: *this man is seriously ill . . .*'

Of course the document mentions neither the nature nor the

consequences of this illness. It does specify, however, that 'He cannot stay much longer in the tropics'.

To which the narrator comments: 'I am not so sure of that.' (1956:65)

The second and third parts of the book show us this structure (the powers and the hero) in action. It is not possible, of course, within the limits of this study, to analyse in detail each of Malraux's novels; once the structure has been outlined, we must proceed by partial touches. The action turns around the efforts of the revolutionaries whose organization is led by two striking personalities, Garine and Borodin – to obtain from the government a decree forbidding ships arriving in China to land at Hong Kong, and thus paralyse the port. The government, which includes not only revolutionary elements but also the representatives of the moderate bourgeoisie, hesitates and equivocates. Now, one of the most important forces of moderation is Chen-Dai, a representative of Chinese tradition, a moralist opposed to violence, whose prestige is considerable. Behind him, stands General Tang, also a member of the Kuomintang, who, with the support of the British, is planning a military intervention against the revolutionary forces in Canton. And Chen-Dai, a supporter of the purely spiritual struggle and of unity in the Kuomintang, supports him, of course, while remaining unaware or pretending to be so that he is thus playing the game of the enemy.

Confronted by them, Hong, the moralist of revolutionary action and violence, is driven to a desire to kill all the rich independently of the political consequences of his action, and without taking into account the fact that the revolutionaries need the support of a section of the democratic bourgeoisie. And by frightening off such support and throwing it into the arms of the moderates, his action will objectively have the same consequences as that of Chen-Dai.

Lastly, it should be added that although the subject of the novel is the victory of the revolutionary forces over General Tang's attempt at military intervention, and although this victory appears in the world of the novel as definitive (all the immediate enemies of the revolution, Tang, Chen-Dai, and even Hong, are defeated and the agreement is signed), it is hinted nonetheless that the struggle continues and that there will still be innumerable episodes like Tang's revolt.

Within this schema, I will select a few episodes that reveal the main characters at work.

Let us begin with Chen-Dai, as he is seen by Garine. His essence is summed up in a word: he is the 'adversary'. His strength finds its source in Chinese attitudes and traditions: 'Just before he died Sun Yat-sen

said: "Borodin's word is my word." But Chen-Dai's word is his also; and
there was no need for him to say so.' (1956:74)

High mindedness is one of the main traits of Chen-Dai's character,
but 'this high mindedness is tinged with a certain shrewdness':

> But the authority he exercises is spiritual, above everything; Garine
> says it is quite right to compare him to Gandhi . . . But though they
> may exercise much the same influence, the men themselves differ
> widely. At the heart of Gandhi's mission is the passionate,
> all-consuming desire to teach men how to live. There is nothing of
> that in Chen-Dai. He wishes to be neither leader nor example, but
> adviser . . . His whole life is a moral protest, and his hope of victory
> is the nearest approach to strength attainable by that profound
> unconquerable weakness which is so common in his race . . . He
> thinks more of his protest than he does of victory. To be the soul
> and the expression of an oppressed people is a part for which he is
> eminently suited (1956:75–77)

Behind him are ranged Tang and the reactionary forces supported by
the British, but when the narrator expresses suprise that 'such a
movement can go on without Chen-Dai's knowing of it', Garine replies:
'He doesn't want to know. He doesn't want to undertake the
responsibility; but I believe he is willing to suspect.' (1956:79)

On the basis of this description, it is easy to understand his interview
with Garine. He has demanded to see Garine and begins by protesting
against the assassination attempts being organized among his friends by
Hong, the moralist of violence. Garine, who is hostile to these attempts,
nevertheless intends to use Hong if necessary against Chen-Dai
himself.[14] For the moment, he is still trying to persuade Chen-Dai to
approve the boycott and to oppose Tang's activities; in this interview,
of course, neither is capable of understanding the other:

> 'Monsieur Garine, I do not think I need ask whether you are aware
> of the acts of violence which have been occurring lately in rapid
> succession . . . Monsieur Garine, these acts of violence are too
> frequent.'
>   Garine makes a gesture which implies: what can I do?
> 'We understand one another, Monsieur Garine, we understand one
> another.'
>   'Monsieur Chen-Dai, you know General Tang, do you not? '
> 'General Tang is a loyal and just man . . . I depend on the Central
> Committee to take effective measures to suppress violence. I believe
> that the best plan would be to accuse publicly all those who are known
> to be leaders to the Terrorist groups.' (1956:86)

The details of the situation now being clear, the discussion becomes ideological:

> Garine: '. . . but you can't doubt the rightness of the course we are taking. All the same, you are trying to thwart us.' 'Your ability, Monsieur Garine, and that of certain members of the Committee cannot be denied. But you act in a spirit of which we cannot altogether approve. For example what importance you attach to the military school of Whampoa!' (1956:87)

Later, he expresses the view that war would not be at all unwelcome to Garine and Borodin and that the Chinese are treated by them as 'fodder for cannon'. Garine objects:

> 'To me it seems that if any nation has been experimented on for the sake of the whole world it is not China but Russia.'
> 'That is true . . . But perhaps she had need of it . . . But we have no right to attack Britain in any overt manner or by any act of the Government . . .'
> 'If Gandhi had not intervened, Monsieur Garine, India, which now offers us the noblest example of our time, would be nothing but an Asiatic country in rebellion.' (1956:89–90)

When the interview is over:

> he rises, not without difficulty, and taking short steps, goes towards the door. Garine accompanies him. No sooner is the door shut than he turns to me:
> 'Great God! Deliver me from saints!' (1956:90)

If Chen-Dai is the moralist of intention, Hong, who is both his opposite and his complement is the moralist of violence and terrorist assassination. How have they arrived at this point? By discovering not a universal principle, but a possibility of existing *qua individual*. Garine explains:

> The poor have understood the helplessness of their condition; they are realizing that a new life has nothing to offer them. When lepers ceased to believe in God they poisoned the wells . . . You will find this exemplified in Hong, and in any Terrorist you may happen to meet. With the new idea of a death which involves nothing, neither compensation nor atonement, has been born the idea that every man has it in his power to overcome the collective life of suffering and to attain to that individual, independent life, which is in some way regarded as the greatest treasure of the rich. (1956:91)

And later, when speaking of Hong:

> he desires neither wealth nor power . . . He discovered that what he
> hates is not the happiness of the well-to-do, but their self-esteem
> . . . Having been led to concentrate on the present by his discovery
> of death, he has ceased to accept, to wonder or to discuss: he merely
> hates . . .

His individualism can be defined thus: he subordinates himself to
nothing and knows no value that supersedes him:

> He does not want order. He will not exchange his present hatred for
> any uncertain future good. He is furious with those who, forgetting
> that this life is all we have, speak of sacrificing themselves for their
> children . . . The frustrator of his vengeance . . . There is no hope yet
> he feels in full vigour . . . An anarchist at heart. (1956:114–15)

And Garine defines his relationship with Hong: 'A break between us is
imminent . . . There are few of my enemies whom I understand better.'
(1956:115)

Although Chen-Dai and Hong are both opposites and analogues, a
moralist of the spirit and a moralist of revolutionary violence, there still
remain to be analysed the two definitions that Garine gives of his
relations with each of them: Chen-Dai is the adversary; Hong, the
enemy, who is closer to him and whom he understands better.

These two phrases would be almost enough to define Garine, for
whom the enemy is, of course, neither Chen-Dai nor Hong but Great
Britain, but for whom they both become the enemy in so far as, in their
behaviour, they objectively aid the adversary and weaken the
revolution. But Garine does not identify himself with the revolution
either; for him the revolution is simply the mediating reality which,
structuring the universe, gives meaning to his action and, therefore, to
his existence.

That is why Chen-Dai and Hong, objective obstacles to the
revolution and, as such, adversaries, are so nevertheless in a different
mode. Chen-Dai, too, is *subjectively* an adversary, for he denies the value
of action and, preaching a universal principle, ignores the problem
of individual authenticity. Conversely, Hong is centred on the same
problem as Garine, that of existing *qua* individual, and chooses the same
means as he does: action and violent struggle against oppression. The
difference between the two lies in that, for Hong, this violence is
enough *qua* abstract reality, whereas Garine, who is also in search of the
meaning of his life, has understood that he can achieve it in an

authentic and honest way only by, on the one hand, ceasing to be preoccupied with himself and, on the other, rejecting any general, and therefore even abstract, idea of it, and rallying to the real forces of history.

Nicolaieff and Borodin, however, can be characterized simply by analysing a particularly important text, the conversation between the narrator and Nicolaieff about Garine. Here Nicolaieff contrasts, in principle, Garine the individualist and Borodin the communist, but he already shows that he does not entirely accept the latter either:

> 'Ah! that Borodin!'
> He puts his hands in his pockets and smiles, but not malevolently.
> 'Much might be said about him.' (1956:161–2)

And when the narrator, contrasting Garine with the Communist Party, speaks of 'Communists of the Roman type . . .', who are defending in Moscow the acquisitions of the revolution and do not wish to accept revolutionaries of the 'conquering type', Nicolaieff corrects him:

> 'You don't understand. Rightly or wrongly, Borodin is trying, as best he can, to represent the proletariat here. His *first* aim is to serve this proletariat, this sort of nucleus that must become conscious of itself, grow in order to seize power. Borodin is a sort of helmsman . . .'[15]

The dialogue then returns to the comparison between Borodin and Garine and we learn that revolution is an axis only as long as it is not a fact (which is valid for both of them) and that Garine in power would run the risk of becoming a *'Mussolinist'*. So we have three human types: Communists of the Roman type (Nicolaieff and the people in Moscow); Borodin who, embodying the revolutionary proletariat, has abandoned all individualism, but for whom the revolution is an axis as long as it is not a fact; and lastly Garine, the individualist who also finds in revolution the meaning of his existence, but for whom the end of the revolution might lead him, if he survived it, to become a Mussolini-type adventurer. This is all summed up in a particularly clear way in Nicolaieff's final words:

> 'It will lead to the unemployment of your "individualist revolutionaries," supported by two resolute Tchekists. Resolute. What is the use of this restricted police force? Borodin, Garine, all that . . .'
> He makes a languid gesture, as if he were mixing liquids.
> 'Borodin will end like your friend. Don't you see that an

independent conscience is a disease in a leader? What we want here is a real Tcheka . . .' (1956:162)

Pursuing my analysis of the world of *Les Conquérants* from the periphery towards the centre, we come at last to Garine.

Garine has found the meaning of his life by committing himself to historical action, in the struggle for the triumph of freedom, and by trying, through this freedom, to leave a mark of his existence in the world of men. The structure of his condition is complex for it cannot be defined, as can that of authentic revolutionaries, Borodin for example, solely, or even primarily, by his commitment in the struggle and his hopes for victory. The meaning of his participation in the conflict is mediatized and results from his desire to give a meaning to his own existence. Garine is above all an individualist and, furthermore, a particular kind of individualist; it is, in effect, the desire to affirm himself *qua* individual in opposition to the permanent and in the last resort inevitable threat – that of annihilation in the *Royaume Farfelu*, in the Empire of Death. This is described in Malraux's earlier works and in *Les Conquérants*,where we are told that Garine had felt both the threat and the presence of such annihilation at the time of his absurd trial in Geneva.

It is his commitment to the Chinese revolution that has brought him something that he has found neither in anarchism, nor in the Foreign Legion – a means of escaping from the absurd. But he has never identified himself with the revolution. Having committed himself in the struggle for a valid cause, Garine is able, through this commitment, to impose on the world by his action the values he holds. However, in order to understand him, it is important to realize that the essential for him is constituted not by values, but by *action*.[16] Now this action is challenged by the ever-threatening intrusion of an inevitable and totally alien reality: death. Death will necessarily and above all *retroactively* deprive his life and his action of all meaning and throw him back into the very void that action had enabled him to escape.[17]

From this point of view, a single sentence indicates the essential axis of the novel, the structure that revolution possesses in it. Garine writes a report intended for Borodin and the narrator comments:

> The Orient and its ancient power loom before me: those Hong Kong hospitals full of patients and foresaken by nurses; and here, scribbling on this paper yellow in the sunlight, one sick man writing to another . . . (1956:113)

In the book, however, illness does not have a static structure. It is constituted by the relation between action and nothingness; its attacks gradually bring Garine closer, in proportion to their seriousness, to death and nothingness. This process continues until the *dénouement*, which will mark the definitive break with the revolution. I shall return to this point later.

It should also be said that the more Garine is committed to action, the more his life attains authentic meaning, so much so that the more he exists the less he thinks of himself, of illness, of death, and of nothingness. At the moment of action, the end to be achieved, the search for victory, the fear of defeat alone occupy his consciousness. Conversely, illness, in proportion to its intensity, brings him back to himself, to death, and carries him away from the revolution.

But absurdity, death, nothingness are abstract concepts, whereas in a novel there are only individual characters and concrete situations. In *Les Conquérants*, they first appear as the memory of the Geneva trial of which Garine is constantly reminded by the attacks of his illness. The absurdity of this trial naturally expresses the absurdity of Western society as a whole and even the society of Asia as it is not in a state of revolution. Indeed, Garine is conscious of this connection between illness and the return to self and the absurd. In the hospital the narrator wants to leave him:

'Would you like to be left alone?'

'Oh, no! I don't want to be alone. I can't bear to think of myself now, and, when I am ill, I always do think of myself . . . It is strange. But after my trial I was obsessed by the vanity of life and of humanity as a whole. It seemed a prey to blind forces. Now this obsession recurs . . . It is idiotic, of course, and comes from my illness. Yet it seems to me that in doing what I am doing here I am struggling against this vanity of life . . . And that it is reasserting its rights . . . Ah! that intangible something which makes a man feel that his life is dominated by some force . . . How strange the power of memory is when one is ill. All day I have been thinking of my trial. I wonder why. It was after my trial that my impression of the futility of the social order came to include everything human . . . I don't see why it should not . . . And yet . . . At this very moment, are there not many who are dreaming of victories which they would have thought impossible two years ago? I am responsible for that dream. I have created that hope. I don't want to preach; but it is hope that makes men live and die. And then? But when one's temperature is high one ought not to talk so much . . It is foolish . . . Yet to lie thinking of oneself all day! . . . Why is my mind fixed on that trial? Why? It was so long ago . . . How stupid fever is . . . But one sees things . . .' (1956:125–6)

Of course, apart from the privileged image of the trial, there are other images that are to have the same meaning. For the moment, we must be content to mention only one particularly important image, both on account of its general meaning and of its insistence in a work in which we meet it for the third time. The image I refer to is that of the fire which, having destroyed the gods that once reigned over the world, leaves today only revolution, which, though not entirely valid (the sick Garine is now moving away from it), remains nevertheless the only promise in which one can still have faith:

> At Kazan, on Christmas night, '19, that wonderful procession . . . Borodin was there, as he always is . . . What? They are bringing all the gods to the front of the cathedral. Huge figures like those carried in carnivals, even a fish goddess in her siren's sheath . . . Two hundred, three hundred gods . . . Luther, too. Players muffled up in furs make the devil of a row with any instruments they can lay hands on. A pile heaped high is flaming. The gods borne on men's shoulders round the square stand out black against the background of fire and snow . . . A roar of triumph . . . The exhausted bearers of the gods throw them on to the flames. A terrific blaze cracks the heads open and shows up the cathedral, white against the darkness . . . What? Is it the revolution? Yes, and this continues for seven or eight hours! I should have liked to have seen the dawn! . . . Corruption, decay! What things one sees! But one cannot cast the revolution into the fire; all that is not the revolution is even worse; one has to admit it, even when one is disgusted. It is just the same with oneself. Neither for nor against. I learned that at the lycée . . . in Latin. It will all be swept away. What? Perhaps there was snow, too . . . What? (1956:126)

There is very little reference to eroticism and even to relations between men and women in *Les Conquérants* (apart from the passage in which Klein's wife finds her husband's corpse, there is only the one scene in which Garine sleeps with two Chinese prostitutes). However, the theme is discussed at length in *La Voie royale*, which was written from the same point of view.

In order to understand these works, it is important, it seems to me, to observe that in Malraux's novels relations between men and women are homologous with relations between the heroes and the social and political world. We have already had the opportunity of observing this in the relations between Klein and his wife, which are ultimately a faithful reproduction of the relations – in so far as they are seen in the novel – between the revolutionary militants, represented by Klein, and the proletariat, or rather, the oppressed, passive people represented by his wife. It is a close, almost organic relation in which the wife and the people feel that the militant is one of themselves even though he does not participate in the struggle, or to be more precise, even though they limit their participation to material aid and to pain when confronted by his tortured corpse.

Similarly, Garine's and Perken's relations with women are analogous to their relations with historical reality, which is to say that they are purely erotic relations. As I have already remarked, Garine and Perken are men of action, conquerors who do not identify themselves with the community of men but use it in order to organize it and to master it and so leave their mark on the universe; for them, women have a function analogous to that of the human group with which they associate themselves — for Garine the revolution, for Perken the Mois. There is created in the erotic relations between them and their partners a community that they direct and in which they are the masters. And this connection in which they treat woman as an object and which enables them to feel that they exist, brings them, on the limited and reduced level of eroticism, the same temporary salvation, the same precarious consciousness of existing, as does, on a much wider level, historical action. This connection makes them feel that they have for a moment avoided the same danger, at once potential and permanent, to which they will necessarily succumb at the end of each erotic scene, and definitively at the end of their lives: nothingness and impotence. The possession of women, above all when it is a psychical possession as in *La Voie royale*, cannot but be provisional. The partner necessarily escapes at the end of the union. Similarly, the prostitutes Garine sleeps with allow themselves to be possessed only provisionally and in an external and fleeting way. This relation is homologous with the one Garine and Perken have with historical reality, which necessarily escapes their domination in the end. They are conquerors, but they are sick, provisional conquerors; eroticism brings them on a limited level what action brings them on a broader, more essential level: the consciousness of existing, an end that can validly be pursued and the possibility of escaping for a time, however brief, from impotence and nothingness.

In order to avoid any misunderstanding, let me stress now that the relations between men and women will be modified in Malraux's later writings in a way parallel with the modification in his over-all vision of man and the human condition.

Lastly, to bring this brief analysis of *Les Conquérants* to an end, let us pause for a few moments at the *dénouement* of the novel, the death of Garine. (I should be careful to mention that the structure of this *dénouement* is taken up again in an almost identical way in *La Voie royale*.) We already know what it consists of: the imminence of death will definitively seperate Garine from the revolutionary movement and hand him back to a solitude in relation to which even the past has lost all real and effective meaning. Having lived throughout the narrative solely in order to ensure the triumph of the revolution, Garine will hear the rhythmic steps of the victorious Red Army with an intense feeling that he is already elsewhere and that there is no longer any real relation between him and the struggle of which this victory is the culmination.

In relation to the classical novel, this end strikes me as both analogous and different. Most novels with a problematic hero in the history of literature end, indeed, with a conversion in which the hero recognizes the vanity of his efforts and his earlier search. Now, the ends of *Les Conquérants* and *La Voie royale* present in certain respects an analogous character. Like Don Quixote, Julien Sorel, Frédéric Moreau, and Emma Bovary, Garine and Perken suddenly feel that their action ceases to bring them authentic meaning and find themselves to be utterly alone. The difference, however, is no less real, in that the quests of Don Quixote, Julien Sorel, Madame Bovary, or Frédéric Moreau had always been vain quests, though the hero was not aware of the fact, whereas revolutionary action remains *in itself* valid, death having merely moved Garine aside and even having retrospectively sullied the validity of his earlier links with it.

Taken with the preceding analysis, these few lines ought to be enough to outline the central function and signification of the hero's death in the novel. It seems to me to be important, however, to stress that, in each of the two works written from this vantage-point, Malraux has chosen the same type of *dénouement* to emphasize to the maximum degree the incompatibility between action and death. Garine is already isolated, snatched from action by the imminence of his death, when he is told that Nicolaieff has just arrested two Chinese who tried to put cyanide in the wells used by the army. Danger brings him back to action and, immediately, by virtue of the same fact isolation and death disappear for a time. They return when Nicolaieff's mistakes have been rectified, the existence of a third agent established, and danger overcome.

Returning to solitude, Garine himself observes the sudden passage from one world to the other: '. . One single blunder at the police station is enough to bring me back to this Canton life; and yet at this moment I feel as if I had left it already . . .' (1956:171)

After that everything is over. To the question, a purely hypothetical one of course, since it is certain he will die at any moment: 'Wherever would you like to go?' (1956:172) Garine replies: 'To England. Now that I know what Empire is – one tenacious, constant act of violence. To direct, to determine, to constrain. That is life.' (1956:172)

But he is already far from Canton and England; he is now on the farther shore of nothingness and its formless kingdom. In a last embrace, the narrator feels the insurmountable abyss that seperates them and the novel ends with the three keywords: Death, Despair, Fraternal Seriousness:

> A strange melancholy springs in me, deep and desperate, inspired by the futility of things and the presence of death. As we seperate and the light shines upon our faces, he looks into my eyes. I search his for the joy which I imagined I had seen gleaming there; I see nothing of the kind, nothing but a hard and yet fraternal seriousness. (1956:174)

It is curious to observe that, as in *Le Royaume farfelu* and *Lunes en Papier*, Malraux has taken up twice in his first novels – with, of course, a number of variations – the same theme: Perken is, in effect, the homologue of Garine, and Claude that of the narrator; the struggle for the defence of the unpacified natives against the constituted States homologous with the Chinese revolt against Britain, and of course, within these two related structures, Perken has the same problems as Garine and offers the same solutions. Although commited to the struggle of the unpacified natives against the organized States – just as Garine is to the Chinese revolution – Perken has not identified himself with these natives, but has found in the organization of their struggle and their resistance to State-imposed civilization the mediating reality that enables him to feel that he exists and to give a meaning to his life.[18]

On the basis of this common structure, there are also a number of differences between the two novels. Just as the two parts of *Lunes en Papier* recount once the defeat and once the victory of the writers in order to show that in each case the fundamental problems remain the same, *La Voie royale* presents, over against the victory of the Chinese revolution in *Les Conquérants*, the defeat of the free tribes. Furthermore, although there is a similarity between the worlds of the two novels, the perspective is different in each case: *Les Conquérants* outlines the over-all structure and shows us Garine at the centre of the struggle between two important groups of historical forces; *La Voie royale* turns the spotlight almost exclusively on the Claude/Perken relationship – the historical forces in conflict are relegated to the periphery of the novel's world and have only an, as it were, abstract reality, just enough to indicate their existence. We will meet in the novel neither the unpacified tribesmen, organized by Perken, nor the government of Siam, although we are aware of their reality and their nature is suggested by the presence of neighbours that resemble them (the Stiengs and the Mois standing for the free tribes, the French administration for the government of Siam). From this point of view, the struggle moves away with the conflicting forces. Its place is taken — partly at least, partly at least, by a number of discussions and conceptual reflections. It is true, however, that these discussions usually concern real, but extremely sketchy aspects of the hero in *Les Conquérants*. This would lead one to suppose that *La Voie royale* was written at the same time as or after the other book and with a certain intended complementarity.

Lastly, there is in *La Voie royale* an apparently new character, Grabot, who has no reality in himself, however, but merely embodies one of the principal dangers that permanently threaten conquerors of the Garine and Perken type.

Having made these preliminary remarks, we need only summarize the plot, pausing to examine on the way a number of particularly significant discussions and scenes.

The general framework of the narrative is the permanent struggle between the formless nothingness embodied by the vegetation of the tropical forest and men's efforts to introduce meaningful forms into it — the Royal Way of the cities and temples that once crossed the desert, but which have since been obscured and defeated by it. Claude and Perken will try to bring these cities and temples back to life, to give them new meaning. Each does this in his own way, one by seeking money, the other by obtaining funds to defend the freedom of the unpacified tribes. On an immediate level, the subject of the novel is the struggle between the desert and the Royal Way — Malraux himself explains that although the work bears this title, it forms only the first volume of a series entitled *'The Powers of the Desert'*.

On a ship bound for Indo-China, Claude meets Perken, a legendary character who has lived for a long time with the unpacified savages among whom he has carved out for himself a kind of empire opposed to the kingdom of Siam and to the territory administered by the French. After a visit to the West, Perken is returning to Indo-China, obsessed and disappointed by an important problem that he has not succeeded in solving: he has failed, in effect, to find the money to buy the machine-guns he needs to carry out his plans.

Psychologically, Perken finds himself in one of those low periods that we have already met in *Les Conquérants* whenever Garine is affected by his illness; indeed, he will explain to us himself that his disenchantment with and his disengagement from action are the result not only of the failure of his attempt to obtain money but also, indeed primarily, of an awareness of old age and the approach of death. In order to characterize the situation, we should also add that, despite his present disposition, in so far as Perken is still thinking of the struggle and of his kingdom, he is preoccupied by the fate of a certain Grabot, an individual like himself, who had set out to carve for himself another empire near his own and whose existence and activity seem to him all the more disturbing in that, for some time, he has disappeared without trace.

Claude's intention is to go to the abandoned temples of the ancient Royal Way and pick up a few statues and bas-reliefs, which he will then sell in Europe for exorbitant sums. A friendship, homologous with that between the narrator of *Les Conquérants* and Garine, is established rapidly and naturally between Claude and Perken. This friendship is based not only on a common need for money, but also on the nature of the two characters: they are both conquerors.

After an encounter, described somewhat satirically, with a civil servant of the French administration, Claude and Perken continue on their way. They do indeed find bas-reliefs in the midst of the tropical forest but, on their way back, they are abandoned by the cart-drivers in country inhabited by unpacified savages. They feel the invisible presence of Grabot. Later, however, they are to discover the truth: having been received into the village by the chief of the savages, they learn that Grabot, who had set out on his difficult and risky enterprise convinced that in the last resort he could always commit suicide, did not have the courage to kill himself and became the slave of the savages. After blinding him, the savages tied him to a mill wheel that he was forced to turn.

Claude and Perken free him and take him to their hut. The Stiengs surround them, angry at such behaviour on the part of their guests. After several hours of extreme tension, during which Perken is wounded in the knee as he falls, a compromise is reached: the Stiengs allow the departure of the two whites, who promise to send them, in exchange for freeing Grabot, one jar for each inhabitant of the village. The promise is kept and Grabot, who is no longer of any interest, is sent to a hospital. But Perken has just learned that his wound is fatal and that he has only a few days to live. Snatched out of the world by his illness, he tries in vain to make contact with the world for the last time in an erotic scene − to which we shall return later. He then learns that the government of Siam, which, in order to subjugate the free tribes, is building a railway, has taken Grabot's mutilation as a pretext to send, together with the jars, a punative expedition against the unpacified natives. Like Garine at the end of *Les Conquérants*, Perken feels the threat that hangs over his work and immediately rediscovers the world of action. Accompanied by Claude, he sets out as quickly as possible for the mountains in order to get there before the government troops and to organize resistance. But death strikes him before he succeeds in his aim — his personal defeat foreshadowing the imminent and inevitable end of his kingdom.

The body of the novel is constituted above all by the struggle of the men — Perken and Claude — against the formless and destructive powers of natural forms. Whole pages might be quoted in support of this, but three short examples will suffice:

> The heat and the never-ending forest harassed them even more than their anxiety. Like a slow poison, the ceaseless fermentation in which forms grew bloated, lengthened out, decayed, as in a world where mankind has no place, wore down Claude's stamina insidiously; under its influence, in the green darkness, he felt himself disintegrating like the world around him. (1935:94)

> Claude was growing aware of the essential oneness of the forest and had given up trying to distinguish between living beings and their setting, life that moves from life that oozes; some unknown power assimilated the trees with the fungoid growths upon them, and quickened the restless movements of all the rudimentary creatures darting to and fro upon a soil like marsh-scum amid the steaming vegetation in the making. Here what act of man had any meaning, what human will but spent its staying power? Here everything frayed out, grew soft and flabby, tended to melt away into its surroundings, which, loathesome yet fascinating as a cretin's eyes, worked on the nerves with the same obscure power of attraction as the spiders hanging there between the branches, from which at first it had cost him such effort to avert his gaze. (1935:95–6)

> Gangrene is as prevalent as vermin in the jungle. (1935:98)

I have already said that the character of Perken presents a structure homologous with that of Garine, a structure in which one finds the same elements: action, eroticism, illness, the threat of nothingness, solitude, death. That is why I have given up any attempt to make a detailed analysis of his character. To do so would mean repeating what I have already said in relation to *Les Conquérants*. Instead, I should like to examine some of the conceptual discussions that occur throughout the work and which enable one to observe, under a magnifying glass as it were, elements that were merely sketched out in *Les Conquérants*.

La Voie royale begins with a long discussion on eroticism, which — and this is not the case in *Les Conquérants* — occupies a particularly important place. This can probably be explained by the author's desire to develop an element that previously he had been content merely to sketch out. But it can also be justified on the psychological and structural level, for if the relations between men and women are on the whole in Malraux's works a reproduction of the relations between men and the world, and if, in the particular cases of Garine and Perken, these relations have a purely erotic character, they also have in their lives a complementary function; whenever disease gains the upper hand and their relations with society and the world are put in question, they try to rediscover the sense of domination and of existence on the more limited, but also more immediate, level of eroticism. Now, in *La Voie royale*, Perken is at just such a low point; this is also why, at the beginning as well as at the end of the novel, at the moment of imminent death, erotic desire comes into the foreground. There is not a great deal to add about the nature of this desire to what I have already said at length in studying *Les Conquérants*. I will merely quote a few phrases by way of|illustration. Perken's eroticism, like that of Grabot (and probably that of Garine had it been brought out into the open), excludes love and is made up above all of a desire for domination and fear of impotence. At the beginning of the book, Perken expresses this in a quite radical way:

A man who's still young can make little or nothing of . . . eroticism. Till he's turned forty he humbugs himself, he can't get 'love' out of his system. So long as he can't see a woman simply as a vehicle of sex, but takes her sexual function as a mere incident of womanhood, he's all for sentimental love — poor devil! (1935:1—2)

The great thing is — not to *know* the woman. She must stand for the opposite sex, no more than that. (1935:6)

Later, Claude remembers an incident in which he had been with Perken in a brothel in Djibouti and which, we learn, 'ended in fiasco'. Indeed, this passage is particularly significant. Perken begins by explaining that he had abandoned action because it was in any case doomed to failure. Without machine-guns, it was impossible to resist the penetration of the Siamese government's railway line. Claude, rather sceptical, thinks the true reason of this abandonment of action lies in the erotic impotence he had witnessed in Djibouti.

Guessing his thoughts, Perken objects that if the two things are true
and can be juxtaposed, the deepest reason[19] for this abandonment is an
awareness of an otherwise irremediable event: the process of ageing that
he had glimpsed through this erotic failure, but which in fact he had
become aware of the first time when observing Sarah, his life
companion.

'So it was considerations of that sort that put you off your scheme?'
'I haven't done with it. If an opportunity comes . . . but I can't
devote my whole life to it any longer. Not that I haven't thought of
it a lot — after that fiasco at the Djibouti brothel, too. Really what's
put me off, as you say, is . . . my failures with women.

It's not impotence; don't run away with that idea. Just a hint, a
menace. Like the first time I noticed Sarah growing old. The end of
something. Above all, I feel my hopes have been drained away, and
some dark force, a sort of hunger, is getting hold of me, fighting me
down.' (1935:86—7)

The same idea occurs later:

. . . But every one bears in mind the fact that — how'm I to make you
see what I'm driving at? — that he may be killed. That's what I
mean. To be killed — that's of no importance. But death, death is
different; it's the exact opposite, in fact. You're too young, of
course; . . . I realized it the first time I saw a woman growing old, a
woman whom . . . well, a woman I knew. (But I've told you about
Sarah, haven't I?) Then, too, as if that warning wasn't enough, there
was that time — the first time — when I found that I was impotent.
(1935:159)

From the same point of view, we learn that Grabot achieves erotic
pleasure only by being tied up and whipped by women, and that he is
terribly humiliated by the fact:

'I told you of a fellow who used to get women at Bangkok to tie him
up naked. That was Grabot. After all it wasn't so very much sillier
than to propose to sleep and live — to live! — with another human
creature. But he feels damnably humiliated by it.'
'Because other people know?'
'Nobody knows about it. Because of himself, because he does it.
So he tries *to make up for it.* That, I imagine, is what really brought
him here. Courage atones for a great deal.' (1935:157—8)

It should be added that the moment he learns that his wound is
fatal, Perken asks for 'women' and although he rediscovers the feeling

of existence at the moment of possession, he soon feels how ephemeral such possession remains:

> ... Frenzied with self-centred passion, her body was withdrawing itself from him irrevocably. Never would he apprehend, never share, this woman's feelings; never could the ecstasy that thrilled her body be for him anything but a proof of the unbridgeable gulf between them. Without love there can be no possession. Carried away by forces he could not control, unable even to make her realize his presence by tearing himself away from her, he too closed his eyes, thrown back upon himself as on a noxious drug, drunk with a wild desire violently to crush out of existence this stranger's face that urged him on to death. (1935:245–6)

Another important and significant passage is the one concerning the distinction between two human types that Malraux sometimes calls the adventurer and the conqueror, but which Claude sees here as corresponding to two modalities of adventure: it resides in the fact that adventurers, while sharing a contempt for the conventions of bourgeois society, think of themselves and of the style of character that they embody, whereas conquerors are engaged in an effective struggle and subordinate everything to the success of a cause that transcends them:

> 'Adventure, as they call it,' he reflected, *'isn't an evasion, but a quest. A break in the established order is never the work of chance; it is the outcome of a man's resolve to turn life to account.'* He knew the type of man for whom adventure is *the food of dreams* — a childish game of make-believe — and he knew, too, that adventure often serves to keep the secret fire of hope aglow. Futilities! (1935:49)

Of Mayrena, Perken says: 'I see him as a player-king, bent on acting his own biography. You Frenchmen usually have a weakness for that sort of man, who prefers *giving a fine performance* to material success.' (1935:9)

'There's a streak of mysticism in every adventurer,' the captain remarks to Claude (1935:16), while Perken would find no pleasure in 'acting his biography', nor would he need to admire his own achievements. (1935:15)

And when he speaks of the difference between Mayrena and himself, Perken adds:

> ... I made a serious attempt to do what Mayrena tried to do, when he fancied himself an actor on the stage of one of your French theatres. Just to *be* a king means nothing; it's the building up of a kingdom that's worthwhile. (1935:83)

Similarly, an important place is given to the figure of Claude's grandfather. Without committing himself to any cause, this man lived isolated and independent, contemptuous of all the social conventions, dying, at seventy-three, 'the death of an old Viking', and Claude, who much admired him, thinks he has found in Perken a similar kind of individual. But Perken himself remarks, 'I suspect that your grandfather was less significant than you imagine, and that you are considerably more so.' (1935:24)

Several passages are devoted to another particularly significant problem: that of suicide, which had already been touched on in *Les Conquérants*, when Chen-Dai is assassinated by Hong, and the assassination is disguised by the victim's supporters as an ideological suicide. At the time, Klein expressed doubts as to the veracity of this suicide with 'inexplicable vehemence', since he cannot believe in the possibility of an ideological suicide:

'I don't approve of suicides.'
'Why not?' Claude asked.
'Every suicide's egged on by a phantom self of his own making; when he kills himself he does it with an eye to survival.
Personally, I'd hate to let God make a fool of me.' (1935:11)

But if suicide is never regarded by the conqueror as a means of combat, its possibility nevertheless remains a decisive element of his consciousness *qua* possibility of avoiding the decline of an existence in which struggle and action have become impossible. Grabot's imposture lies specifically in the fact that he had wanted to live and act as a conqueror, whereas at the decisive moment he did not have the courage to kill himself. Let me say in passing that his weakness was already foreshadowed in the paragraph quoted above concerning his peculiar relations with eroticism. On this subject, there is a particularly significant scene in the book: surrounded by the Stiengs, Claude considers the possibility that he and Perken should kill themselves with their last bullet if they do not manage to get away:

He tapped the cartridge in the magazine. 'There'll always be two left.'
'Wha-at?', a harsh voice drawled.
Grabot had spoken at last. Only one voice could have put such concentrated venom into a single word — the voice of the blind man besides them. There was more than bitterness in it; a deep conviction, too. Startled, Claude turned and looked at the man again. His skin was a cadaverous grey, the complexion of a dweller underground, but he had a wrestler's shoulders. A wreck, but a

mighty wreck. And he had once been more than brave. But, as on the temples, Asia had set her mark on him; he, too, had fallen on evil days. Yet this man had had the temerity to destroy one of his eyes, and to explore these perilous regions without the least safe-conduct. 'At the worst things can't go further than the muzzle of my revolver.' No less than the Mois Grabot inspired him now with infinite horror.

'But, blast it all, surely a man can . . .!'

'Bloody fool!'

More eloquently than the insult, and even than his voice, the jerk of Grabot's mutilated head conveyed his meaning. 'You can't when its unnecessary, and when it's necessary – it may be too late to act.' (1935:191–2)

To bring to an end this enumeration, which could of course be made much longer, I would like to point out a number of passages in *La Voie royale* concerning the meaning of life, and the *dénouement* of the novel, which is similar in every way to that of *Les Conquérants*.

For Perken, as for Garine, the meaning of life lies in action as the only way of overcoming the threat of nothingness, impotence, and above all death. Let me quote, by way of example, the dialogue with Claude on the ship, at a moment when, exhausted, Perken has decided to abandon action:

'By the way, what will the journey's end mean – for you?'

'Doing things instead of dreaming them. And, for you, what . . .?'

'Wasting time.' . . .

'Will you be going among the unpacified tribes?'

'I shouldn't call that "wasting time"; quite the contrary.' . . .

'The contrary?'

'I've found out pretty nearly everything that's to be found up there.'

'Everything except money, you mean?' (1935:33–4)

And later:

'It's not I who choose; it's something in me that resists.'

'Resists what?'

Claude had put the question to himself often enough to be able to give a prompt reply.

'The idea of death.'

'Death, the real death, is a man's gradual decline . . . Yes, *growing old is infinitely worse.* Having to accept one's destiny, one's place in the world; to feel shut up in a life there's no escaping, like a dog in its kennel! A young man can never know what death is.' (1935:47)

Or again:

> He might be killed, might disappear – it mattered little to him, for
> he had small interest in his own survival – yet, thus at least, he
> would have found his fight, if not the victory. But, living, to endure
> the vanity of life gnawing him like a cancer; all this|life|long to feel the
> seat of death lie clammy in his palm . . . What was his quest of the
> unknown, the slave's brief spell of freedom from his master, that men
> who do not understand it call adventure – what was it but his
> counter-attack on death? (1935:50)

> Ah, could he but shake off the wearisome inertia of the voyage, this
> tyranny of dreams and hopes deferred! (1935:53)

The structure of the *dénouement* is homologous with that of *Les
Conquérants*, which proves the extent to which Malraux intended
explicitly or implicitly to convey to his readers the relations between
the consciousness of death and action in the structure of the characters
of Garine and Perken.

Isolated, alone in the face of death, Garine had forgotten death in
order to throw himself back into action for the brief period of the
interrogation of the two enemy agents who had tried to poison the
wells, only to find, of course, that once the episode was over he sank
back into an ever deeper soltitude. The reason for this episode seems
obvious enough: it is intended to convey to the reader the extent to
which participation in action, even when this action is quite obviously
provisional, doomed to last no more than a few moments, excludes by
its very presence any return into oneself, any thought concentrated on
illness, solitude, death.

Similarly, when Perken, conscious of his imminent death and of the
vanity of any attempt to forget himself in eroticism, suddenly learns
that *his* tribes are threatened by the advance of the government's
troops, and throws himself back into action, this consciousness will lose
all importance even all reality, although he knows that he is
irremediably condemned. The text says this explicitly: Savan, the chief
of one of the unpacified tribes, would like to postpone the battle with
the government forces. Perken, who talking with him, speaks to Claude
in French:

> But by then, *perhaps,* I shall be dead!'
> Yet, amazingly, the tone of his voice belied the words; faith in his
> life had returned to him. (1935:266)

A little later, when they are threatened with having the road cut:

'There are moments,' he murmured, as if he were talking to himself, 'when I feel the whole damned business hasn't the least importance.'

'Our being cut off, you mean?'

'No. Death.' (1935:273)

But the illness takes its course and death is inevitable; Perken, forced to become aware of it, first tries to bind it to action:

'Damn this fever! When I'm through with it, I'd like at least . . . Do you hear me, Claude?'

'Yes, old chap. I'm listening.'

'Well I'd like to feel my death had . . . forced their freedom on them.'

'What can that matter to you?'

Perken shut his eyes wearily. Hopeless it was, trying to make another human being understand! (1935:275)

Then, as the illness progresses, action fades away and is replaced by solitude; Perken would still like to get home and die where his existence had found meaning, even if this meaning has become alien to him:

He knew that, though in his own country *he might have recovered, here he must die.* On the little nucleus of hopes that was his very life the world would set its stranglehold, clamping those iron tracks upon it, like a prisoner's chains. And nothing in the universe could ever compensate him for his past and present sufferings; to be a living man was even more absurd than dying! (1935:276–7)

He will die however in the world of the absurd and nothingness, having become alien to everything around him, including Claude and his own body:

And Claude was here beside him, Claude who would go on living, who believed in life *as some believe their torturers are human* . . . Claude, too, was hateful now! *Alone. Alone* with his fever coursing between his head and knee, alone with the one thing loyal to him yet – his hand, lying upon his thigh . . .

Nothing would ever give a meaning to his life – not even this sudden ecstasy that merged him in the sunlight. Men walked the earth, men who believed in their passions, their sorrows, their own existence – . . . And yet no man had ever *died;* all had but drifted into nothingness like the smoke-clouds yonder dissolving into air, like the forest and the temples. He, only he, would die, be wrenched out of the scheme of things . . .

'There is . . . no death. There's only . . . I . . . I who . . . am dying.'

With a rush of hatred Claude recalled a prayer of his childhood. 'O Lord, be with us in our last agony . . .' Ah, could he but express by look or gesture, if not by words, the desperate fraternity that was wrenching him out of himself! He passed his arm round Perkin's shoulders.

Perken gazed at him as if he were a stranger, an intruder from another world. (1935:276–84)

On the subject of *Les Conquérants,* we have two documents of great interest, not only because of the exceptional personalities of their authors, Trotsky and Malraux, and because of the problems they pose, that of revolutionary strategy and that of the relations between politics and literature, but also because it is very possible that this discussion played a fundamental role in the development that led Malraux from *Les Conquérants* and *La Voie royale* to *La Condition humaine,* where the Trotskyist point of view occupies a considerable place.

Trotsky, who had read *Les Conquérants* two years after its publication, saw it above all as a political document of some importance and had sent an article to the *NRF* (*Nouvelle Revue française*) in which he assesses the work from this point of view. It would be difficult to imagine a deeper failure to understand the literary aspect of the work. From the beginning of the article, after observing that Garine is Malraux's spokesman, he writes that 'the book is called a novel'. 'In fact,' he emphasizes, 'we are confronted by a fictional chronicle of the first period of the Chinese revolution, the Canton period.' Later, he speaks of Malraux's 'novel', taking care to put the word in inverted commas. This shows to what extent Trotsky, imprisoned in his politician's outlook, misses the properly literary structure of the work, which is in fact a novel *without inverted commas* and the hero of which is Garine and not the revolution.

Having made his position clear, a position already very familiar from his other writings, that of the revolutionary proletariat that must commit itself to an *offensive* policy, opposed to all compromise and all the political forces of the bourgeoisie, Trotsky develops his critique on the basis of Malraux's description of the Chinese revolution. The situation in China seems to him to be analogous with the revolutionary situation that had developed in Russia in October 1917. I should observe in passing that he criticizes Malraux among other things for having made Borodin a revolutionary whereas in reality Borodin was merely a Komintern bureaucrat who had taken part neither in the 1905 nor in the 1917 revolution. (I refer to this for, in *La Condition humaine,* Borodin will indeed appear as a mere party bureaucrat.)

Malraux's much shorter reply falls into two parts and operates on two different levels. In the first, he rightly explains to Trotsky that his work is a novel and not a chronicle of the revolution: 'This book is not a "fictional chronicle" of the Chinese revolution because the stress is placed on the relation between *individuals and a collective action,* not on collective action alone.'

He then goes on to treat seperately what, in Trotsky's criticism, 'is born from the conditions of fiction', that is to say derives from the need to resolve an aesthetic problem that Trosky had not even noticed. In this sphere pride of place is given to the character of Borodin who, though perhaps a bureaucrat from Trotsky's point of view, appears as a professional revolutionary to Garine and his followers. In short, 'the viewpoint of the novel dominates the novel'. But, having said this, and since even Trotsky recognizes that the characters have 'the value of social symbols', Malraux also tackles 'the discussion of the essential', that is to say, the political problems posed by Trotsky.

This second part of the reply is a forceful, if respectful, defence of the policy of the International. Trotsky does, in fact, confuse the situation in China and in the world with that of Russia in 1917. Although the offensive tactic was perfectly justified in a position of strength, a position of weakness requires on the contrary a defensive tactic of the kind carried out by the Communist International at the time the events described by *Les Conquérants* took place. On this point, it should be noted that although, in the first part concerning aesthetic and literary problems, Malraux was entirely right against Trotsky, who missed the main point, he is also no doubt right, in part at least, when he deals with the political problems. The great difference between the policy advocated by Trotsky and the policy chosen and carried out by the Communist International was in fact the difference between an offensive and a defensive policy corresponding, respectively, to an optimistic assessment and a pessimistic assessment of the existing balance of forces. But Malraux describes the policy of the Communist International as if it were solely an assessment of the situation in China and of the problem of a *provisional* temporization, intended to allow a building up of the available forces for a new offensive, whereas in reality the opposition between Trotskyism and the policy of the International, which later became the policy of Stalin, was much deeper and international in character. Even the phrases used by the two opposing groups expresses this clearly enough. Each saw the opposition between offensive and defensive as no doubt important, but as *derivative* of another deeper opposition: that between the strategies of the 'permanent revolution' and of 'socialism in one country'.

Trotsky knew that the balance of forces was not always favourable to the revolution, but he thought that socialist society could not be constructed in a backward country like Russia without being supported by an international revolution, and he saw in the policy that he advocated the only hope of increasing the chances of the success of the revolution and of the survival of socialism in the USSR.

The leadership of the International, on the other hand, set out from the idea that the essential factor was to preserve the already established Soviet bastion and that in view of the unfavourable balance of forces emerging from the stabilization of capitalism (the phrase then in use was 'relative stabilization'), any revolutionary movement ran the risk, unless it spread over a large part of the world and was victorious, of creating an anti-Soviet international coalition and of placing the very existence of the USSR in jeopardy. It is on this basis that the various stages of the defensive policy have been developed, from the Stalin/Bukharin period, during which even greater stress was laid on the alliance with democratic and pseudo-democratic forces (in China with the Kuomintang and implicitly with Chiang Kai-shek), to the Stalin period, when an absolutely defensive policy was advocated that led to the Non-aggression Pact with Nazi Germany in 1939, and which involved the use of the apparatus of the International and of the Communist parties against any development and deepening of the revolutionary movement that might arise anywhere in the world.

If I have touched on these problems here, it is because they seem to me to be of vital importance for an understanding of Malraux's next novel, *La Condition humaine*, which we will now examine. The subject of this novel is the Chinese revolution and, more particularly, the conflict between, on the one hand, the Shanghai group of revolutionaries and, on the other hand, the leadership of the Party and International which orders them not to resist Chiang Kai-shek, and between the two values embodied by these forces: the Trotskyist value of the immediate *revolutionary community* and the Stalinist value of *discipline*.[20]

Appearing after *Les Conquérants* and *La Voie royale*, this third novel was to have an enormous impact and made Malraux famous throughout the world.

Although it is still what I have called one of the 'transitional' novels (between the novel with a problematic hero and the novel without character), and although the subjects is still, as in *Les Conquérants*, the

Chinese revolution, the world of *La Condition humaine* is, in relation to the two preceding novels, entirely different.

Was the author influenced by his discussion with Trotsky? It is, of course, impossible to establish this with any certainty. Nevertheless, the work is in certain respects — but *only in certain respects* — fairly close to the Trotskyist point of view.

But however important an element the 'chronicle of the revolution' is (and it is much more important in *La Condition humaine* than in *Les Conquérants*, it remains, in the final resort, of secondary importance for a structuralist or even a merely literary analysis. The true novelty of the book lies in the fact that, in relation to the worlds of *La Voie royale* and *Les Conquérants*, which were governed by the problem of the hero's individual realization, the world of *La Condition humaine* is governed by quite other laws and above all by a different value: *that of the revolutionary community.*

Let us approach the essential point at once: as a novel in the strictest sense of the word, *La Condition humaine* has a problematic hero, but , as a novel of transition, it describes for us, not an individual but a *collective problematic character:* the community of Shanghai revolutionaries represented in the narrative primarily by three individual characters, Kyo, Katow, and May, but also Hemmelrich and by all the anonymous militants by whom we know they are surrounded.[21]

A *collective* and *problematic* hero; this characteristic, which makes *La Condition humaine* a true novel, derives from the fact that the Shanghai revolutionaries are attached to the essential and, in the world of the novel, contradictory requirements: on the one hand, the deepening and development of the revolution and, on the other hand, discipline towards the Party and the International.

But the Party and the International are engaged in a purely defensive policy. They are strictly opposed to any revolutionary action in the city, withdraw the troops that are faithful to them, and demand the handing back of arms to Chiang Kai-shek, although, quite plainly, Chiang is planning to assassinate the Communist leaders and militants.[22]

In these conditions, it is inevitable that the Shanghai militants should turn to defeat and massacre.

In so far as the book is *also* a 'chronicle of the revolution', one sees why its point of view is *fairly close* to the thinking of the Communist opposition. It is written from the point of view of Kyo, May, Katow, and their comrades and implicitly stresses the sabotage of their struggle by the leadership of the Party and the responsibility of this leadership for the defeat, massacre, and torture of the militants.[23]

In this framework, the value that governs the world of *La Condition humaine* is that of the *community*, which is, of course, the *community of the revolutionary struggle*.

Since the world in which the action unfolds is the same as that of *Les Conquérants*, the characters – with a few minor exceptions – are necessarily the same, though they are seen from a quite different point of view. So, in order to illuminate them more clearly, it might be useful to analyse them in turn, situating each of them in relation to the corresponding character of the preceding novel.

We will begin, of course, with the main character: the group of revolutionaries. In *Les Conquérants*, it was personified by Borodin.[24] The difference is obvious enough, but it is justified by the difference of perspective.

As seen by the individualist Garine, the revolutionary can only be *an individual* whose distinctive feature is the fact that he is not only closely linked to the proletariat and to the organization that directs the revolution, but also that he goes so far as to identify himself with this proletariat and this revolution, whereas, *seen from the inside*, this distinctive feature is specifically what transforms the individual into a community. So the story related in *La Condition humaine* is not only that of the action carried out by Kyo, May, Katow, and their comrades, the history of their defeat and death, but also, closely bound up with this action, the history of their community, which is a living dynamic psychical reality.

Around them, if we leave to one side certain incidental figures, we will meet four characters who belong to no community and who remain more or less isolated individuals: an ally, the Chinese terrorist Chen, an an enemy, Ferral, and two intermediary characters, Clappique and Gisors.

I have just written 'an *ally*, the Chinese terrorist Chen', whereas in *Les Conquérants*, Hong remained in spite of everything an *enemy* whom Garine – in spite of all his sympathy – was finally to execute. The difference derives from the fact that, far from being Hong's homologue, Chen is a mixture of Hong and Garine, a mixture in which the elements related to those that made up the personality of Garine are predominant. This is explained and, indeed, justified by the same difference of perspective. Seen with Garine's eyes, the difference between him and Hong was considerable. Hong, in effect, has an abstract attitude, alien to any concern for efficacity, whereas Garine could find meaning – however precarious and provisional – in his existence only in revolutionary action entirely subordinated to the *efficacity* of the struggle.

From Borodin's point of view, however, this difference loses much of its importance. Hong and Garine resemble one another in so far as they are both individuals who, though declared and active enemies of the bourgeoisie, nevertheless do not identify themselves with the revolution.

On the side of the enemies of the revolution, only one character is really present in the novel: Ferral, who directs an industrial consortium, helps to overthrow Chiang Kai-shek's alliances and organizes the agreement between Chiang and the Shanghai bourgeoisie. He is a character of the *conqueror* type but, of course, a much more superficial conqueror than Garine and Perkin, since instead of rallying to the revolution he has committed himself to the side of false values, to what, in the novel, embodies evil and lies. In fact, he really represents one of the risks to which this human type is exposed, a risk that had been touched on in *Les Conquérants* by Nikolaieff when he suggested to the narrator that Garine might have become a 'Mussolinian'.

Lastly, between the revolutionaries and reaction, two characters in the novel occupy a fairly important position: Gisors, Kyo's father, and Clappique. Clappique is an old acquaintance who had disappeared from Malraux's two preceding novels. He personifies the aerostats and deadly sins of *Lunes en Papier*, the man who lived in imagination; the nonconformist artist, the buffoon. It should be said, however, that at the time he was writing *La Condition humaine,* Malraux had much more sympathy for him than at the period of *Lunes en Papier.* This, too, can be explained: *Lunes en Papier* is an attempt to unmask people who claimed to be only valid revolutionaries in a world in which there was no place for hope, whereas now Clappique, between the revolutionaries on the one hand, and Chiang Kai-shek or Ferral on the other, acts more or less as a sort of gadfly. Nevertheless, we must admire a writer who, despite his sympathy for Clappique, is quite merciless in showing that his attitude of detachment from reality, while useful at times, may also be detrimental, even fatal, to the revolutionaries fighting for authentic values.

Gisors embodies the old Chinese culture, which is, in the last resort, alien to all violence, whether reactionary or revolutionary. In relation to *Les Conquérants*, he really corresponds to Chen-Dai. But he is a very real character and this correspondence is more complex and more mediatized than in the case of the other characters. Chen-Dai was opposed on principle to revolutionary violence. Gisors, on the contrary, is bound to the revolution not directly — for ideological reasons — but out of affection for his son[25] who is committed to it body and soul. Now it seems to me that we have here two *complementary* aspects of old China and it would be impossible to imagine Gisors in *Les Conquérants* or Chen-Dai in *La Condition humaine.* Nevertheless, there is a structural reason in favour of the solution adopted by Malraux: *Les Conquérants* describes the victory of the revolution, *La Condition humaine* its defeat. Now it is of the essence of the Gisors and Chen-Dais of this world to be opposed to victorious violence and to find themselves, rather ineffectively no doubt, on the side of the defeated.

The plot of the novel, although poignant and tragic, is simple enough: faced with the advance of the Kuomintang army (which *still* comprises both Chiang Kai-shek and the Chinese Communist Party) the clandestine organization of the Shanghai Communists, supported by the trade unions, is planning an uprising intended both to facilitate the victory of the attackers and, at the same time, to get control of the leadership of the movement *after* victory. In fact, the conflict between Chiang Kai-shek and the Communists became increasingly sharp as the victory of the Kuomintang became imminent. Having been united in a struggle between a common enemy, they will now have to solve the problem of the social and political structures of the new China that the defeat of its enemy will leave as the major problem.

An important section of the militants of the Chinese Party, and among them, the Shanghai revolutionaries, organized the peasants and unions by promising to the first agrarian reforms and to the second the seizure of power in the towns. In order to resist them and to maintain control of the Kuomintang, Chiang Kai-shek plans to form an alliance with his former enemies, break with the Communists, and massacre the militants. The leadership of the International and Chinese Communist Party decide that they are too weak to engage in the struggle and forbid any revolutionary action. They allow Chiang Kai-shek a free hand, in the hope that this timorous attitude will lead Chiang to think that repression of the Communists is pointless and to maintain his previous policy, or, at least, to postpone the break with them.

The Shanghai militants, who are already fully engaged in action, are rightly convinced of the contrary. For material as well as ideological reasons, however, they cannot act in isolation and in opposition to the Party leadership. So they are left with no option but to face defeat and massacre. The novel recounts their action just prior to the entry of the Kuomintang into Shanghai, their reactions on learning the decisions of the Party leadership, their defeat after Chiang Kai-shek's entry into the city and, lastly, the torture and massacre of the Communists by Chiang's men – a massacre in which, among many others, two of the novel's three heroes, Kyo and Katow, are killed.

The work begins with a famous scene: Chen's assassination of an arms dealer, or, to be more precise, an agent, in order to get from him a document that will enable the revolutionaries to gain possession of a number of pistols. This assassination reveals at once the difference between Chen and Hong: on the psychological plane, it is an act that will help Chen to become aware of his personal problems; on the material level, it is an act ordered by the revolutionary *organization* and therefore forms part of an *organized* action. There is a passage in the book that indicates both the importance of this assassination for the collective struggle and the particular meaning it has for Chen himself:

> The approaching attempt to place Shanghai in the hands of the revolutionaries would not have two hundred rifles behind it. If the short carbines (almost three hundred in number) which the dead entrepreneur had just arranged to sell the Government were thrown in too, the chances of the rebels would be doubled, for their first step would be to seize the arms of the police for their own troops. But during the last ten minutes, Chen had not once thought about that.[26]

Having carried out the murder, Chen has to walk through the hotel, where life continues its usual way. The episode leads to a remarkable description of the opposition between two qualitatively different worlds: that of revolutionary action and that of an everyday life indifferent to ideas and politics. In *La Condition humaine*, this opposition serves to indicate Chen's awareness of the difference between the world of terrorist action to which he belongs and that of 'the life of men who do not kill'. Some years later, in *Les Noyers de l'Altenburg*, Malraux was to use a similar description to indicate Victor Berger's discovery, in Marseilles, at the time he was abandoning the struggle for the victory of *Ottomanism* (for which, I believe, one should read *Communism*), of the existence of the world of everyday life that is indifferent to ideas and action, in which however unattached he may be, he fails to become integrated. Chen, meeting a 'Burmese or Siamese by the look of him, and rather drunk', who says to him 'the little piece in red is an absolute peach!', wanted 'both to strike him, to make him hold his tongue, and to embrace him because he was alive'. In *Les Noyers de l'Altenburg*, only the opposition between the two worlds, that of action and that of everyday life, is emphasized. In *La Condition humaine*, on the other hand, there is added, by way of opposition, to the everyday life that is indifferent to politics and the world of terrorist action that isolates, a third world whose development constitutes the essential subject of the novel: that of the revolutionary community, to which Chen's action partly belongs and whose function and aim are precisely to integrate the two others. After the murder of the agent and the walk through the hotel full of indifferent merrymakers, Chen returns to his comrades:

> Their presence was breaking down Chen's ghastly feeling of isolation. It yielded gently, like an uprooted plant which still clings to the ground with a few slender threads. And as he gradually drew nearer to them it seemed to him that he suddenly knew them for the first time — as he had known his sister after his first visit to a brothel. (1968a:10)

I have said that Chen corresponds much more to the character of Garine than to that of Hong and that, in the last resort, he is a synthesis of the two. As for Hong, his first assassination will be an intoxication, a decisive turning-point in his life. Like Garine, however, he will return after the assassination to the organization of revolutionary militants that Hong was never to see again, and never at any point in the novel does he come into opposition with that organization. Like Garine, too, he works within the collective struggle, but does not identify himself with it.[27]

Having returned, after the assassination, to the group of revolutionaries, Chen meets among his comrades two characters who are at the centre of the novel, not so much as individuals, but as representatives of the entire group, of the revolutionary community — Katow and Kyo.

What characterizes each of them is their total commitment to action. In the book, Katow will be seen only as a militant in the struggle, at the moment of his arrest, then of his execution. Kyo, on the other hand, will be seen also in his private life, in his relations with May. But this does not represent the addition of a new, different sphere, for May and Kyo are characterized by the organic synthesis of their public and private lives, or, to use Lukacs's expression, by the total synthesis of the individual and the citizen; and precisely because, in everyday life, this synthesis — which did not exist in Malraux's earlier writings either — is extremely rare, it is important to stress the extent to which Kyo's thinking and consciousness are *entirely* engaged in action. Moreover, Malraux will tell us on several occasions that Kyo's entire thinking was organically structured by the imminent struggle.

One such moment is when he is entering the Chinese quarter, after deciding to attack the boat and take the pistols:

> 'A good quarter', thought Kyo. For more than a month he had gone from one meeting to another, organizing the rising, oblivious of the existence of streets: what was mud to him beside his plans? . . .

As he turned out of a narrow passage he suddenly found himself looking down one of the main streets, wide and well-lit. Despite the rain beating down, which half obscured its outlines, he never for a moment saw it save as something flat which would have to be attacked in the face of rifles and machine-guns, firing horizontally. (1968a:15)

Another moment occurs when he has crossed the Chinese quarter and reached the gates of the Concession:

Two Annamese troopers and a sergeant from the Colonial army came and examined his papers. He had his French passport. As a tempation to the guards, hopeful Chinamen had stuck little pies all over the barbs of the wire. ('Good way of poisoning a station, if need be', thought Kyo). (1968a:18)

Once inside the Concession, he looks for Clappique. As I have already remarked, Clappique lives not in reality, but in imagination. This is expressed among other things by his external appearance: whatever he was wearing — tonight he was in evening clothes — Baron Clappique looked as if he were in disguise. (1968a:20)

He finds him drawing an imaginary picture of Chiang Kai-shek for the benefit of two dancing-girls. How does he see himself in this picture?:

'And what'll *you* find to do?'
     He whimpered: 'Can't you guess, dear girl, do you mean to say you can't guess? I shall be Court astrologer, and one night when I am drunk — can it be tonight? — I shall meet my death digging for the moon in a pond!' (1968a:20)

I shall come back later to the two other characters to be examined here — Gisors and Ferral.

What defines *La Condition humaine* in relation to the previous novels is first of all the absence of the element that was the most important in those works, the principal characteristic of Garine, Perkin, and even Borodin — illness. Illness does exist, of course, in *La Condition humaine*, but only to the extent that the work *also* is in part a social chronicle: illness among the children of the poor, the consequences of an unsuccessful suicide attempt by a woman who wanted to die in order to avoid being married to a rich old man, etc. As revolutionary militants, the heroes themselves may be massacred and tortured, but they remain nevertheless essentially healthy; one might even go so far as to say that they define, by their existence, the summit of the human condition and, therefore, the summit of health. If there is disease, it concerns, not the individuals, but the revolutionary collectivity that is the true hero of the novel and whose problematic character I have already remarked on. It would not be possible here to study the psychology of this community step by step, so we shall approach it from two particularly important points of view: love and death, the relations between Kyo and May on the one hand, and, on the other, the torture and execution of the revolutionaries after Chiang Kai-shek's victory.

Love and death are, in effect, two important elements in characterizing fictional characters in general and particularly those of Malraux. In *La Condition humaine*, however, they have a different nature and function from those that they had in the previous works. I have already said that, in Malraux's world, relations between men and women always reflect the over-all relation between men and the world. That is why, in the world of Perken and Garine, we met only eroticism and relations of domination, whereas in *La Condition humaine*, a novel of the authentic revolutionary community, eroticism is, like the individual, integrated and superseded in an authentic, higher community: that of love.

In *La Voie royale* one sentence alone hinted at the possibility of the relation that was to be at the centre of *La Condition humaine*. I have already quoted it: at the moment when Perken, learning of his imminent death, takes refuge in a final erotic fling, at the moment he becomes aware of the impossibility of any lasting erotic possession, he also realizes that 'one possesses only what one loves'.

These words, *which have no meaning in the world of La Voie royale*, *where love is non-existent*, prefigure *La Condition humaine*, in which Malraux was to create with Kyo and May the first pair of lovers in his *oeuvre* and one of the most beautiful, purest love stories in major twentieth-century fiction.[28]

Eroticism and domination are not, of course, totally absent from the work — there are even justly famous scenes of this kind, but they involve, not Kyo and May, the heroes of the novel, but the subsidiary character of Ferral, who as I have already said, corresponds in certain respects to Garine/Perken. In addition, though in a more human context, we also find in the character of Chen, who is also to a large degree reminiscent of Garine, the same pure erotic relationship with women.

However, between the eroticism and domination of the previous novels and the same relations in *La Condition humaine*, there is an important difference — one that is essential for the understanding of the characters. In the earlier novels, eroticism and domination constituted precarious, but positive values, whereas they are entirely modified, even devalued by the very presence of love in this novel of the revolutionary community. I shall return to this. Let us begin however with the love of Kyo and May which is, in *La Condition humaine*, a story of love in the twentieth century, a period in which such a feeling is no longer accessible to every man or woman. That is why it can be successful only in so far as it is organically linked to the revolutionary action of the two partners.

The story of this love is that of an entirely new feeling that comes into conflict with the relics that still exist in each of them of a type of feeling and eroticism that they have in fact superseded. In other words, Kyo and May cannot always live up to their own existence and the weakness that survives in each of them will finally be overcome only through action and imminent death, which help them and force them to rediscover their own levels.

The facts are well known: knowing that their relationship allows each of them both to preserve his own freedom and to respect the freedom of the other, May in a moment of exhaustion – and, partly also, moved by the pity and solidarity that binds her to a man who she knows will run the risk of being killed in a few hours – has slept with a comrade, even though she did not love him. Convinced that this is of no importance in her relations with Kyo, which on the contrary would be affected by the slightest lie, she tells Kyo about it. Kyo feels intense pain and an acute feeling of jealousy:

Kyo felt pain in its most degrading form; pain which his self-respect dare not admit. In point of fact she was free to sleep with whoever she wished. What then was the cause of his suffering for which he could find no justification, but which held him in such complete subjection? . . .

'Kyo, I'm going to tell you something strange, but true. Until five minutes ago, I thought you wouldn't mind. Perhaps it suited me to think so. There are some things people ask of one, above all when death is as near as this (it's other people's death that I've had to face till now, Kyo . . .) which have no connexion with love . . .'

Jealousy there was, notwithstanding; all the less clearly perceived in that the desire which she awoke in him was based upon affection. His eyes closed, and, still leaning on his elbow, he set himself the painful task of understanding. He could hear nothing but May's laboured breathing and the scratching of the puppy's paws. The principal cause of his suffering (he would inevitably find others: he could feel them lying in ambush, like his comrades who still waited behind their closed doors) lay in his idea that that man who had just slept with May ('I can't after all call him her lover') despised her. The man in question was an old friend of hers, whom he hardly knew; but he knew well enough the contempt in which women were ultimately held by almost all men. 'The idea that having slept with her, as a result of having slept with her, he may be thinking: "That little tart"; I could kill him for that. Are we always only jealous of what we imagine the other person is thinking? Men are pretty hopeless creatures . . .' As far as May was concerned, sexual relations implied no kind of contract. That ought to be made clear to this man. If he slept with her, well and good; but don't let him start thinking he possessed her. ('This is becoming pitiable . . .') But that was something out of his control – and he knew that, in any case, it wasn't the vital thing. The vital thing, the thing which was torturing him almost beyond endurance, was the barrier which had suddenly cut him off from her: it wasn't hatred which had done it, though there was hatred in him: it wasn't jealousy (or perhaps that was just what jealousy was?): it was a feeling to which he could give no name, as destructive as Time or Death: he could not recapture her. (1968a:39–40)

And Kyo leaves without relations between them returning to normal:

May offered him her lips. In his heart Kyo wanted to kiss her; not her mouth, though – as if there alone bitterness still lingered. He kissed her at last, clumsily. She looked at him sadly, with listless eyes which suddenly filled with animation as the muscles regained control. He left her. (1968a:42)

It is only when he is alone in the street again, involved once more in action, that he realizes how deep their love is:

'What have other men in common with me? Just so many entities who look at me and criticize. My real fellow-creatures love me unreflectingly, love me in spite of everything, love me so that no corruption, vileness or betrayal has any power to alter it: love me for myself and not for what I have done or will do; whose love for me goes as far as my own – embracing suicide. . . . With her alone do I share a love like that, whatever batterings it may have undergone, as others share the sickness of their children, their risk of death . . .' It certainly wasn't a feeling of happiness, it was something primeval, in tune with the darkness, which set him tingling till he stood there locked in an embrace, as if his cheek were laid against another – the only part of him which was stronger than death.

On the roof-tops, vague shapes were already at their posts.
(1968a:43–44)

The crisis is overcome only at the moment of defeat, when Kyo sets
out for the meeting of the Central Committee; he knows, as does May,
that he will probably be arrested and executed. At first, however, the
tension seems to accumulate:

Where are you going?'
   'With you, Kyo.'
   'What for?'
   There was no reply.
   'We shall be more easily recognized together than seperately,' he
said.
   'I don't see why. If you're on their list, nothing is going to make
any difference . . .'
   'You can't do any good.'
   'What good should I do waiting here? Men don't know what
waiting is like.'
   He walked a few steps, then stopped and turned towards her.
   'Listen, May: when it was a question of your freedom, I gave it
you.'
   She knew what he was alluding to, and it frightened her: she had
forgotten it. She was right, for he went on, dully this time:
   '. . . and you took advantage of it all right. Now it's mine that is
involved.'
   'But, Kyo, what has that got to do with it?'
   'To recognize someone else's right to liberty is to acknowledge
that that is more important than one's own suffering: I know that
from experience.'
   'Am I just "someone else", Kyo?'
   He remained silent. Yes, at that moment, she was. A change had
taken place in their relations.
   'You mean that because I . . . well, because of that, in future we
can't even face danger together? Think, Kyo: one would almost
imagine this was a kind of revenge.'
   'Not to be able to any more and to try to when it's useless are
quite different things.'
   'But if it rankled as much as that, you could perfectly well
have taken a mistress. At least, no: that's not true. Why do I say
that? I didn't take a lover, I just went to bed with somebody. It's not
the same thing, and you know quite well that you can sleep with
anyone you want.'

'I'm satisfied with you,' he answered bitterly.

May was rather puzzled by the way he looked at her. Every possible feeling seemed to enter into his expression. What made her feel really uneasy was the quite unconscious lust which was apparent in his face.

'As far as that goes,' he went on, 'my feelings are the same now as they were a fortnight ago: I just don't want to. I'm not saying that you are wrong, but that I want to go alone. You acknowledge my liberty; you possess the same degree of liberty yourself. Liberty to do what *you* please. Liberty isn't a bargain, it's just liberty.'

'It's a desertion.'

Silence.

'What is it that brings people who love each other to face death, unless it is that they can face it together?'

She guessed that he was going to leave without further argument, and placed herself in front of the door.

'You shouldn't have given me this liberty, if we have to be separated now as a result.'

'You certainly didn't ask for it.'

'You had already given it me.'

'You shouldn't have believed me', he thought. It was true, he had always given it. But that she should discuss rights now, that widened the gulf between them.

'There are some rights which one only grants,' she said bitterly, 'so that they shall not be used.'

'If they had been granted so that you could hang on to them at this moment it wouldn't be so bad . . .'

In that second they were drawing even farther apart than in death. Eyelids, mouth, temples, a dead woman's face still shows the site of every caress, whereas those high cheekbones and elongated eyelids which confronted him then belonged to a foreign world. The wounds of the deepest love suffice to create a thorough hatred. Was she so near death that she was recoiling from the animosity which she had seen preparing? She said:

'I'm not hanging on to anything, Kyo. Say I am making a mistake if you like, that I've already made one; say what you please, but just at this moment I want to go with you; now, at once. I beg you.'

He didn't answer.

'If you didn't love me.' she went on, 'you wouldn't think twice about letting me come. Well then? Why cause us unnecessary suffering?'

'As if this were a good time to choose', she added wearily . . .

'Are we going?' she asked.

'No.'

Too honest to hide her impulses, she reiterated her desires with a cat-like persistence which often exasperated Kyo. She had moved away from the door, but he realized that all the time he had wanted to pass through he had been sure that he wouldn't really do it.

'May, are we just going to leave each other quite suddenly like this?'

'Have I behaved like a woman who expects protection?'

They stood there face to face, not knowing what else to say, and not content to remain silent, conscious at once that that moment was one of the most solemn of their lives, and that it could not endure – that time was already corrupting it: Kyo's place was not there, but with the Committee, and a certain impatience lurked all the time at the back of his mind.

She nodded towards the door.

He looked at her, took her head between his hands and drew it gently towards him, without kissing her; as though in that firm embrace he had somehow projected all the mingled tenderness and ardour of which masculine love is capable. At last he withdrew his hands.

The doors shut, one after the other. May continued to listen, as if she were expecting to hear a third one close, brought into existence by her imagination. Her mouth hanging limply open, wild with grief, she was beginning to realize that if she had signed to him to leave, it was because she saw in that movement the one final hope of persuading him to take her with him. (1968a:164–8)

But, once in the street, Kyo again feels the strength that unites him to May:

Parting had not relieved Kyo's distress. The reverse was the case: May seemed all the stronger in this deserted street – after yielding to him – than when she had been fighting him face-to-face. He entered the Chinese town, aware of the fact, but quite indifferent to it. 'Have I behaved like a woman who needs protection?' What right had he to extend his pitiable protection to this woman who had submitted even to his leaving her? *Why* was he leaving her? Was it perhaps a kind of vengeance? No doubt May was still sitting on the bed, broken by despair which no reasoning could alleviate.

He turned and ran back.

The phoenix-room was empty: his father had gone out, May was still where he had left her. He stopped in front of the door,

overwhelmed by a feeling of the friendliness of death, and yet
conscious of how, despite its fascination, his body recoiled grimly
before the unnaturalness of the contact. He understood now that to
be willing to lead the women he loved to her death was perhaps love
in its most complete form, the love beyond which nothing can go.

He opened the door.

Without a word she hurriedly threw her cloak around her
shoulders, and followed him out. (1968a:169)

When they arrive at the meeting-place, May is knocked unconscious
and Kyo arrested. Later, when he's about to be executed, he swallows
the cyanide that most of the revolutionary leaders carried with them
for just such an eventuality, thus killing himself in order to avoid
torture. At the moment of death, he rediscovers unreservedly, and in
their entirety, both May and all his comrades in the struggle:

Kyo shut his eyes . . . He had witnessed death on many occasions
and, aided in this by his Japanese upbringing, he had always felt that
it would be beautiful to die a death that is one's own, a death
appropriate to the life it closes. And to die is passive, but to kill
oneself is to turn passivity into action. As soon as they came to fetch
the first of his lot, he would kill himself in full consciousness of
what he was doing. He remembered the gramophone records and his
heart dropped a beat: in those days hope still had meaning. He
would never see May again, and the only hurt he felt was the hurt
that she would feel – as if he were doing something unkind, and
wrong, in dying. 'Death brings remorse,' he thought, with a twinge
of irony. He felt no such qualms for his father, who had always given
him an impression not of weakness, but of strength. For more than a
year now May had protected him from all loneliness, though not from
every sorrow. There sprang into his mind, alas, as soon as he thought
of her, the remembrance of that swift refuge in tenderness of body
joined to body. Now that he was no longer to be numbered among
the living . . . 'She will have to forget me now.' Could he have
written to tell her so, he would only have been torturing her and
tying her closer to him. 'And it would mean telling her to love
another . . .' Oh, this prison – a place where time stops still, while
elsewhere it runs on. (1968a:252–3)

Compared with this total union between Kyo and May, in which one
can dissociate in no way the private relationship from the revolutionary
activity, compared with this *realized totality*, the other relationship
between man and woman decribed in the novel, that between Ferral
and Valérie (there are only a few references to Chen's erotic relations

with prostitutes) is naturally devalued and degraded; and it is hardly surprising if this devaluation necessarily involves in *La Condition humaine* a change of nature. There is no longer any domination, any predominance on the part of the man. Valérie revolts and, in order to humiliate Ferral, arranges to meet him in the hotel lounge at the same time as another meeting she has arranged with a character of the same world — each man having been instructed to bring a canary. Valérie does not turn up at the rendez-vous and the two men find themselves face to face, ridiculous, accompanied by their servants carrying the cages with the birds.

By way of revenge, Ferral fills Valérie's room with birds. We do not know what happens afterwards — and we hardly care. The relationship has lost all interest.

And yet, in *Les Conquérants* and *La Voie royale*, this relationship of erotic domination was, on the level of the private life, the very value that enabled Garine and Perken to assert themselves and to feel their own existence.

In addition to love, death is the other event that constitutes the existence of the main characters in the novel. In my comments on the moment when Kyo swallows the cyanide and feels May's presence in an unusually intense way, I pointed out the significance and function that death has for the revolutionaries of *La Condition humaine*, a significance and function different and even opposed to those that it had for Garine and Perken in the earlier novels. In *Les Conquérants* and *La Voie royale*, death was the inevitable reality that rendered precarious and provisional all social values bound up with action, which annihilated them *retroactively* and brought the hero back to the formless, to absolute solitude, whereas in *La Condition humaine* it is, on the contrary, the moment that realizes in its entirety an organic union with action and a community with the other comrades. In the preceding novels death broke all links between the individual and the community. In *La Condition humaine* it ensures the final supersession of solitude. Among the characters embodying the revolutionary group itself, two deaths have already been described for us, those of Katow and Kyo. I have already spoken of the latter: Kyo is to die, reunited not only with May, but also with Katow, his comrades, and above all the very meaning of his struggle and his existence. That is why his death is not an end: his life and his struggle will be taken up again by all those who continue the action after him:

> He would die having fought for what in his own day would have possessed the strongest meaning and inspired the most splendid hope; die, too, among those whom he would wish to have seen live;

die, like each of these recumbent forms, so as to give significance to his own life. What would have been the value of a life for which he would not have accepted death? It is less hard to die when one is not alone in dying. This death of his was hallowed by a touch of common brotherhood, by contact with a gathering of broken men whom future multitudes would recognize as martyrs, whose bloody memory would bring forth a golden hope! How, already staring into the eyes of death, should he fail to hear the murmur of human sacrifice calling aloud to him that the heart of man is a resting-place for the dead, well worth the loss of life itself? . . .

No, dying could become an action, an exalted deed, the supreme expression of a life to which this death was itself so similar; it meant, too, escape from these two soldiers who now uncertainly approached him. He jerked the poison between his teeth, as he would have barked an order, heard anguished Katow still asking him something, felt him stir and touch him; then just as, gasping for breath, he tried to clutch him, he felt his whole strength slip, fading from him, giving way before the onrush of an overwhelming convulsion (1968a:253–4)

Similarly, Katow's death is the moment at which he is reunited in the most intense way with the revolutionary community. Beside him, two Chinese militants are lying full length, terrified by the whistle of the locomotive into which Chiang Kai-shek has the prisoners thrown alive. Katow, in an act of supreme fraternity, gives them his cyanide. Unfortunately, one of the Chinese is wounded in the hand and drops it. For a few moments it might be thought that Katow's act had no efficacy. But beyond the material reality, fraternity is stronger and more present than ever. His two Chinese comrades no longer feel alone:

Their hands brushed against his. Then suddenly one of these hands seized his hand, clutched it, held it fast.
'Even if we don't find anything,' said one of the voices, 'still . . .' (1968a:257)

But the cyanide is found again, and his two comrades escape torture. Katow is led to the train. It is perhaps the most intense and solemn moment in the novel. He goes through the scene surrounded by the fraternity of all the other prisoners, wounded, bound to the ground, and destined to the same fate:

The torch-flare now showed him in even blacker silhouette against the windows that looked out on to the night. He walked heavily, slumping first on one leg, then the other, hampered by his wounds; as he staggered towards the glare of the torch, the shadowed outline of his head merged into the roof. The entire darkness of the hall had come to life and watched him step by step. The silence now was such that the ground rang at each heavy tread of his foot. Nodding up and down, every head followed the rhythm of his walk, tenderly, in terror, in resignation, as if, although all the movements were the same, each man would himself have struggled to follow these faltering footsteps. No head fell back as the door closed.

A sound of deep breathing, like the sound of sleep, came up from the ground; breathing through the nose, jaws clenched in anguish, not stirring now, quite still, all those who were not yet dead waited to hear the shriek of a distant whistle . . . (1968a:258–9)

It becomes obvious that the subject of *La Condition humaine* is not only a chronicle of the events in Shanghai; it is also, indeed primarily, this extraordinary realization of the revolutionary community in the defeat of the militants and their survival in the revolutionary struggle that continues after their death. And, of course, it is in relation to this struggle that the later destiny of the other characters is situated. Two of them, Hemmelrich and Chen, will be brought back into the struggle. The former had hesitated all his life between his duties to his wife and child, passive victims, incapable of defending themselves in a barbarous and unjust world, and his revolutionary aspirations; he will be freed by the repression which, murdering those dearest to him, gives him back the freedom he had always dreamed of and enables him to commit himself entirely to action.

Chen, who was supported unofficially by the group of revolutionaries, tried twice to organize an assassination attempt on Chiang Kai-shek. He is cut to shreds during the second attempt and kills himself. At the moment he throws the bomb, he finds himself entirely alone and when he dies he is aware that in this world 'even the death of Chiang Kai-shek can no longer affect him'. This is, on the immediate level, the death of Garine and Perken, but at the end of the novel we learn that his disciple Pei, through whom he had hoped to ensure the continuity of his anarchist action, has set out for Russia and joined the communists. Thus Chen's very act and total solitude into which he found himself thrown back at the moment of death have been superseded and integrated by historical action.

Three characters leave the orbit of action: Gisors, for whom Kyo's death broke all links with the revolution, returns to the passive pantheism of traditional Chinese culture; Ferral is ousted from action by a consortium of bankers and civil servants who take over his work[29]; Clappique is forced to hide from the repression that is directed at him in so far as he helped Kyo and disguises himself as a sailor — a disguise in which he finds the true meaning of his life.

There remain the combatants, May, and, behind her, Pei and Hemmelrich, about whom something more should be said. The novel tells us simply that all three went to the USSR, where they continue the struggle, and that they will later come back to China, the construction of the USSR, the realization of the five-year plan having become 'the main weapon of the class struggle' for the moment.

Malraux's ideological position at the time he wrote the novel, therefore, was not Trotskyist, but, on the contrary, fairly close to the Stalinist positions. Nevertheless, the two chapters that express his position, namely the twenty odd pages of Part III that take place in Hankow, and the last six pages of the book, are much more abstract and schematic than the rest of the novel, and appear to some extent as an afterthought or foreign body.[30]

If the unity of the novel does not suffer from this, and if *La Condition humaine* remains a powerfully coherent and unified novel, it is above all because these fragments scarcely add up to a tenth of the work; moreover this tenth is not entirely devoted to expressing this ideological position.

In fact, Malraux's explicit ideology has an insignificant place in *La Condition humaine*, whereas the unorthodox point of view of the Shanghai revolutionaries constitutes the unifying point of view from which the novel is written. Nevertheless, in each of these two passages, Malraux is forced to make the transition between two almost irreconcilable positions. He does this in the chapter that takes place in Hankow by referring to 'all the hesitations' of Vologuin, the representative of the International. These doubts are expressed in the fact that, while declaring himself to be opposed to any assassination attempt on individuals, and in particular against the attempt on Chiang Kai-shek proposed by Chen, Vologuin nevertheless lets Chen go, thus encouraging his terrorist action.

Malraux also makes this transition at the end of the work in the psychology of May who, going over to the side of the Party and the International, becomes integrated in a struggle that must in principle absorb and integrate that of the Shanghai revolutionaries. May is going, we are led to believe, to begin a new life, but she does so 'without enthusiasm', with a heavy heart and, quite obviously, without having resolved her problems: ' "I hardly ever weep now, any more", she said with bitter pride.' (1968a:283)

In *Les Conquérants* and *La Condition humaine*, Malraux wrote the first two French novels of the proletarian revolution of the twentieth century. He did not identify himself however with the Communist Party that directed this revolution. Indeed, we have seen that the fundamental values that structure the worlds of these two works are different from those of the Party, although the Party represented, in each case, a positive value and, quite obviously the transition from the novel of Garine to that of the community of the Shanghai revolutionaries constitutes an important step towards a revolutionary perspective.

Compared with these two novels, *Le Temps du Mépris* and *L'Espoir* mark an important change: the total acceptance of the Communist Party.

It should be stressed, however, that the structure of the world is not homologous in the two works.

Le Temps du Mépris is an account of one episode in the revolutionary struggle, a struggle that makes possible human dignity, an immediate community and the reconciliation of man with the world — the Communist Party being *naturally* and *implicitly* valued in so far as it organizes and directs this struggle. In *L'Espoir*, however, the Party is *consciously* valued as the organization that realizes the military discipline of the struggle *against* the spontaneous aspirations of the people in general and of the proletariat in particular.

One might, it seems to me, characterize in the following way the four novels that have the proletarian revolution as their subject:

Les Conquérants is the novel of the relations between *the problematic individual*[31] — Garine — and the revolution that enables him to give, in a provisional and precarious way, an authentic meaning to his existence.

La Condition humaine is the novel of the relations between *the problematic community* of the Shanghai revolutionaries, who, as individuals, have *definitively* found an authentic meaning for their existence in struggle and defeat, and the totality of revolutionary action within which the tactic of the Communist International makes their death and defeat inevitable.

Le Temps du Mépris is the account of the *non-problematic* relation of the individual Kassner with the *non-problematic* community of revolutionary fighters and, implicitly, the Communist Party which is part of it and directs it.

Lastly, the subject of *L'Espoir* is the *non-problematic* relation of the Spanish people and the international proletariat with a Communist Party that is disciplined and opposed to spontaneity.

This enumeration raises at once two kinds of question. There is the question of the transition from a position of distance in relation to the

Communist Party to its *unreserved* acceptance and there is the question of the disappearance of the problematic hero, and, with it, of the strict novel form.

The first question appears at first sight to concern the biography and psychology of the author — and on this I do not feel that I can throw any light. It is by no means certain, however, that it does not involve a much more general phenomenon that goes beyond the mere biography of the writer. *La Condition humaine*, published in 1933, was written before that year; *Le Temps du Mépris* belongs to 1935. Between the two works occurred the Nazi seizure of power in Germany, which had profound repercussions in the intellectual and political circles of the European Left. Many militants thought that after this seizure of power, the demands of the anti-fascist struggle forced them to place less importance on the reservations they had about the Communist Party. This was made all the easier in that the Party abandoned the theory and policy of 'social-fascism' and, from 1934 onwards, adopted the policy of the anti-fascist struggle and the Popular Front.

Faced with the rise of Nazism just prior to 1933, two other important figures in the intellectual life, Georg Lukács and Ilya Ehrenburg — to confine ourselves to the internationally known names of the independent Left and the Communist opposition — joined Malraux in adopting the official positions of the Party. And in 1933, one of the leaders of the Russian opposition, Christian Rakowsky did the same.

Of course, this closing of the ranks, which, apart from the four internationally known names mentioned above, also applied to several thousand little known or unknown militants, took on a particular meaning in each individual case — each of these militants having more or less explicit reservations about the 'official' line. But to take only the four names mentioned, it is obvious that the two theoreticians, Lukàcs and Rakowsky, had much stronger reservations, on the explicit level of their writings and their professions of faith, than did the writers Ilya Ehrenburg and Malraux.

We should study much more closely, therefore, the repercussions of the development of Nazism and Hitler's seizure of power on Marxists and para-Marxists if we are to appreciate the extent to which Malraux's development is a matter of mere biography or the expression of a deeper tendency corresponding with certain currents in the collective consciousness.

On the level of literary form, it seems to me that the disappearance of the problematic hero leads naturally to an abandonment of strict novel structure; thus, neither *Le Temps du Mépris* nor *L'Espoir* are novels in the narrow sense of the term, but forms somewhere between the epic and the lyric.[32] In these works the absence both of the delicacy of the epic poem and of the structured 'story' of the novel tolerates only the form of the brief isolated or repeated episode that alone can avoid both incoherence and abstraction.

This is why, it seems to me, *Le Temps du Mépris* became a *novella* and *L'Espoir* a series of apparently loosely linked episodes.

Le Temps du Mépris is made up of three closely related parts, but for all that it is not a novel. This work might be characterized as a *novella* tending to the lyric. I have already formulated the hypothesis that the shortness of the narrative and its lyrical character derive from the gap between the subject intended, the total unity of the individual and the community, and the real content of the book, in which this unity appears only as the final result of a struggle in the course of which it is threatened on several occasions; (whereas the epic poem proper could bear no threat of this kind).

As Lukács has said, 'The epic poem knows only answers but no questions', and Malraux's story is largely that of a question that stands as a permanent threat throughout the book, even if in the end it is overcome. It is really, if I may use the term, a pre-epic narrative situated at the moment when, as Malraux says, 'a god' or, what amounts to the same thing on the level of literary criticism, the epic poem *is about to be born.*

Fortunately, we possess a particularly important text on the nature and world of this narrative, namely, Malraux's own short preface to the book, which also serves as a sort of literary manifesto.

In his preface, Malraux shows that he is aware that this work places him at a turning-point between two forms of narrative literature: that of the novel with an individual, problematic hero and that to which his new work belongs and which he calls, wrongly in my opinion, tragic, whereas in reality it is simply concerned with a world in which man can achieve total, non-problematic greatness, by creating and maintaining an organic link with the community.

Although the term 'tragic' seems to me unsuitable, I do think, however, that Malraux is right, fundamentally, when he distinguishes these two literary forms as being, on the one hand, that of the individualism of such nineteenth-century writers and artists as Flaubert or Wagner, directed above all towards the inner world and individual differences, and, on the other hand, a form to which, rightly or wrongly, he links the names of Aeschylus, Homer, Chateaubriand, Nietzsche, and even Dostoievsky, a form that attempts 'to give men a consciousness of their own hidden greatness'.

L'Espoir, of course, belongs to the second category.

Thus having situated his work in a sort of historical typology of fictional forms, Malraux enumerates the constitutive elements of the world of a work which, he tells us, has only two characters, '*the hero and his sense of life*', and it is not concerned with the individual antagonisms that give the novel its complexity — these elements are '*man, the crowd, the elements, woman, destiny*'.

This is a valid analysis, I think. It is worth noting that one of the main constituent elements of the world of the first novels, death, no longer appears and that Malraux was right to omit it both from the list given in the preface and in the body of the work, in the sense that — as I have already said in the first part of this study — when the individual manages to insert himself in an organic way in a world governed by supra-individual values, death loses — whether these values are transcendent or immanent, whether they relate to god or to the human community — its primordial significance, if not its empirical reality.

I should like to point out two more particularly important ideas expressed in this preface:

a) The world of man organically linked to the community, the world of rediscovered unity, which can no longer be centred upon the psychology of individual differences and the originality of the hero, necessarily becomes in our time a world of *action and struggle*.

b) Describing the humanity of the *Communist militant Kassner,* and having broken therefore with the writers of the eighteenth and nineteenth centuries, Malraux thinks he has rediscovered the tradition of the great period when individuals were integrated in the totality, the tradition of the Christian person, the Roman Empire, and the soldiers of the Rhine army.

To sum up this introductory text is already to outline the essential structure of a world that Malraux characterizes as that of *virile fraternity*.

Let us now examine the narrative proper.

The book tells the story of the Communist intellectual Kassner who, having decided to enter a house surrounded by Nazi police in order to destroy a list of names that a careless comrade had left there, is arrested and taken to a concentration camp. He is then freed through the intervention of another militant who, either spontaneously or under orders from the Party (we never learn), takes his place and gives himself up to the police under his name. He returns to Prague where he finds his wife, his child, and his other comrades, with whom he resumes the struggle.

The three episodes that make up the narrative are respectively those of the concentration camp, the flight in the plane, and his arrival in Prague.

Malraux told us in his preface that the book has only two characters: the hero and his sense of life. This is true as far as the essential theme of the work as seen *from the point of view of the hero* is concerned. But the sense of life is identified for the hero by the weakening or maintenance, at the most critical moment (the moment at which he is locked up in a cell and abandoned to the Nazi brutes), of his links with the revolutionary community (embodied in this book, as it is not in Malraux's other works, including *L'Espoir, naturally* and *unproblematically* by the Communist Party).

What is at issue, therefore, is the extent to which the virile fraternity that binds Kassner to his comrades and, through them, to mankind and the world, can remain intact in the solitude of the camp, in the face of policemen who are about to torture him, who may at any moment kill him, and who will probably do so, when he has nothing to oppose them with but the scarcely credible appearance of his false identity and the strength of his physical and moral resistance. This resistance has nothing to do with the individualistic attitude of the Stoic setting his autonomy against the reality of the human and natural world; it is based solely on an awareness of the community of other men. This ability always to feel at home in the world weakens and tends to disappear when the individual feels alone and alienated.

The key sentence of the narrative comes to Kassner in a dream, in which it is spoken by the Tartar caravaneers under the Mongolian sky: '. . . *and if this night should be a night of destiny – May it be blessed until the coming of dawn* . . .'[3][3] For, in his cell, he too is plunged into a night that may for him be a night of destiny and, although, like the caravaneers he is sure of the future arrival of the dawn, he is, like them, not at all sure that he will be there to see it.

Will he, in this situation, have the strength to take up the words of the caravaneers, to accept events, whatever they may be?

The entire first part of the work is a continual oscillation between a feeling of abandonment and solitude and a feeling of the presence of the virile community of combatants.

This oscillation is determined in the first instance through the immediate atmosphere and through the attitude of his body. When he hears his gaoler's steps in the distance, the sound of their blows in the cell next door, the groans of his tortured comrade, he feels alone and weak; but when the gaolers arrive in his cell and start to beat him, his resistance becomes firmer and his vital strength returns to him again:

Later, he is left alone once more and, after a few moments during which 'his first sensation was one of comfort', Kassner feels his will crumbling again:

> His strength, grown parasitic, was gnawing him relentlessly. He was an animal of action, and the darkness was draining his will-power.
>
> He must wait. That was all. Hold out. Live in a state of suspended animation like the paralysed, like the dying, with the same submerged tenacity — like a face in the very heart of darkness.
>
> Otherwise madness. (1936:42)

Similarly, when during an attack of weakness he wants to commit suicide and reflects on how long it would take him to sharpen his nail against the wall so that it might serve in opening his vein, his gaolers only have to throw a rope into the cell in the hope of inciting him to suicide for all his strength to return and for his only real concern to be whether in the neighbouring cells other comrades are likely to give in under pressure from the torturers.

When in his solitude he suddenly experiences a terrifying and undeniable fear that his wife is dead, that she has abandoned him, he has to react, to walk a few times around his cell, to become convinced once more that she is alive and that their community continues to exist.

The presence of comrades is also expressed in the prison through his efforts to make contact with the other prisoners by knocking on the walls, through the knockings made by his neighbour in reply and which he finally comes to decipher, through the importance that this understanding assumes, through the awareness of the fraternity that binds him to this comrade, who is discovered by the guards and taken away. It is also expressed in the writing left on the walls by those who were incarcerated before him, writing in which they tell of their dejection, their courage, their determination to persist in the struggle and to which he adds his own, addressed individually to each prisoner: '*We are with you.*' (1936:35)

Between the two terms of this alternative — depression, the threat of nothingness and madness, on the one hand, and, on the other, courage, acceptance of one's destiny — the final decision will depend ultimately on the fact that Kassner will or will not be able to keep alive within himself an awareness of the struggle being waged throughout the world, and which has been waged, in particular, in the revolution in which he once participated, by all those to whom he is bound in a virile fraternity that alone can give meaning to man's existence. He pictures the enemy to himself as 'a vulture shut up with him in a cage, which with relentless blows of its pick-shaped beak was tearing off pieces of his flesh, all the while staring greedily at his eyes'. (1936:50)

This vulture flies away whenever, in his dream, the internal music that flows through him revives the spirit of struggle and fraternity. He sees the militants, wounded, killed, or, on the contrary, victorious; he thinks of the coldness and inhumanity of this world against which he struggles with them, a world that condemns men to spiritual impoverishment and solitude; he sees the endless procession of Young Communists on Red Square, a procession that lasts over seven hours and in which thousands of young men and women take part who, thanks to the revolution, have never experienced the hardships of the struggle and have never known the days of contempt; he sees Lenin dead in Red Square and hears the words of his wife at his funeral: 'Comrades, Vladimir Ilyitch deeply loved the people . . .' (1936:100)

And when the gaolers take away the neighbour who used to knock on the wall, when he feels once again the threat of solitude, he finds support in his struggle against it in that other ultimately triumphant reality: the fraternity of those who in these days of contempt are struggling throughout the world against the barbarians:

> Deprived of brotherhood as he had been of dreams and hope, Kassner waited in the silence which hung over the desires of hundreds of men in that black termites' nest. He must speak for them, even were they never to hear him!
> 'Comrades in the darkness around me . . .'
> For as many hours, as many days as were needed, he would prepare what could be told through the darkness . . . (1936:96)

And this fraternity finds expression in its highest form: a man whom Kassner does not know has given himself up − perhaps spontaneously, perhaps on the orders of the Party − to the police, declaring that he is the Kassner they are looking for. By allowing himself to be killed in Kassner's place, he enables Kassner to return to freedom and the struggle.

The second part of the narrative consists of the flight into Czechoslovakia. Kassner knows that he will not be free − if only to return later to Germany under another identity − until he has crossed the frontier. The underground organization provides him with a plane and a pilot; however, the sky is overcast and a storm is imminent. Nevertheless, they must leave at once and, once again, a man, a comrade, will risk his life in order to save him and to bring him back where he is needed − in the fraternity of the struggle.

The remarkable description of the struggle between the plane and the storm is, quite obviously, influenced by Saint-Exupéry.[34]

That is why it seems to me to be interesting to analyse what Saint-Exupéry's flight scenes and Malraux's first scene in an aeroplane have in common and where they differ. Essentially, it seems to me that in Saint-Exupéry it is the struggle between natural obstacles that creates the virile fraternity of the combatants and the unity between them and nature, setting them against the petty world of pen-pushers and bureaucrats, whereas in Malraux it is the virile fraternity in the struggle for freedom — symbolized here by the struggle against the hurricane — that blossoms into universal fraternity and cosmic pantheism.

In the plane, at the height of danger, Kassner feels in this struggle against all the unleashed forces of nature that his surest support is still the same fraternity that binds him, first to the pilot, then to all those who throughout the world, in prison, under torture, are waging the same struggle:

> It suddenly seemed to Kassner that they had been released from gravitation, that they were suspended with their comradeship somewhere among the worlds, caught in the clouds in primitive combat, while the earth and its prison cells, which they would never meet again, continued their course beneath them. The frantic clinging of the tiny mechanical contrivance to the unbridled clouds, in the darkness surrounding the fuselage on all sides, was growing increasingly unreal, and at the same time all sensations were being submerged beneath the primitive voices of the hurricane. (1936:127)

The third part of the narrative recounts Kassner's arrival in Prague, where he rediscovers everyday life, men in the street, work, the hands that make all the objects that one uses. He buys a packet of cigarettes and tries to rejoin his wife and child; but he finds the house locked; a message on the door tells him that Anna has gone to a meeting for the liberation of the anti-fascists imprisoned in Germany.

During his worst moments of depression, he had believed her dead, had believed himself separated from her. In fact, she had never ceased to struggle for him and with him.

At the meeting, he meets hundreds of men and women and, more than once, thinks he recognizes Anna among them.

A man had sacrificed himself for him; another had risked his life to enable him to get here; thousands of men were struggling for his liberty and that of all men: 'Oh, how absurd to give the name of brothers to those who are merely of the same blood!' (1936:145)

Here he rediscovers in the true fraternity, the fervour of the crowd, 'which surrounded Anna also . . . their reply to the challenge of that body beaten to death against the wall of the cell'. (1936:156)

He had often asked himself what value thought had when faced with the death of the individual: 'No human speech went so deep as cruelty. But man's fellowship could cope with it, could go into the very blood-stream, to the forbidden places of the heart where torture and death are lurking . . .' (1936:157)

Later, on returning home, he finds Anna and their child once again and, aware both of the intensity of their union and of the fact that it exists only through their common participation in the wider fraternity of all those who struggle for the dignity of man against oppression, Kassner and Anna will repeat together the solemn prayer of the Mongolian caravaneers:

'And if this night should be a night of destiny . . .'

She seized his hand, lifted it to her forehead; and, pressing her face against the back of it, she murmured:

'. . . may it be blessed until the coming of the dawn . . .'
(1936:173)

In characterizing this culminating moment of the narrative, Malraux takes up one of the key images of his fictional *oeuvre*, that of the life or death of the gods, an image, however, that takes on in this new context a new aspect and a new significance: for the death of the gods is substituted their birth: 'One of those moments which make men believe a god has just been born flooded the house . . .' (1936:174)

Having obtained at last this summit of plenitude, not only of this work in particular, but perhaps, too, of the whole of Malraux's fictional *oeuvre*, a moment that is born out of a fraternity free of any concern for originality and egoism, Anna and Kassner feel that they cannot remain alone and isolated, that they must go out and meet the others, the essential basis, the nourishing soil of their existence:

'I feel like walking, like going out with you – anywhere!' . . .

They were now going to speak, remember, exchange experiences . . . All this would become a part of everyday life, a stairway which they would descend side by side, into the street, with the sky eternally looking down on the defeats or victories of men's wills. (1936:175–6)

La Condition humaine and *Le Temps du Mépris*, the two novels of the revolutionary community, are also in Malraux's *oeuvre* the only works in which one finds two human beings who love one another. This, of course, is both natural and coherent, since love is the expression in the private life of the authentic community of men. For the same reasons it is understandable that in this world of the revolutionary community both couples should be militants, that both the man and the woman should participate, together, in the struggle. Indeed, on this point, the difference between Saint-Exupéry's and Malraux's humanism can be brought out particularly clearly. Malraux's conquerors — Perken, Garine, Claude — do not experience love and reject it, but when love appears in this *oeuvre* it is that of two equal beings participating together in the struggle for freedom. Saint-Exupéry's characters, on the other hand, have an aristocratic, conservative structure. They are medieval knights linked to the modern technology of aviation. They feel love as an essential element of their existence. The woman they love is what binds them to life, what enables them to come through the worst ordeals and prevents them each time from giving up. And yet, in spite of everything, this woman remains an inferior, if idealized, being, since none of these heroes would allow her to participate actively in their struggle. Fraternity and love are, in Saint-Exupéry's *oeuvre*, complementary and essential realities, situated on different levels, whereas in Malraux's two novels they are situated on the same level.

But let us return to the revolutionary community in Malraux's *oeuvre* and to its complement — love. We know that both meet in *La Condition humaine* and *Le Temps du Mépris*. A difference in the nature of the community in the two novels involves, however, a homologous difference in the nature of love.

The Shanghai revolutionaries constitute, as I have already said, the *problematic* community, with no future, which, while giving a definitive meaning to the life of each of its members, can lead them only to defeat and death.[35]

Thus the love of Kyo and May is a deep, intense love that cannot be surpassed, but it has no future and ceases with them. Neither Kyo nor May can, for reasons that concern the aesthetic coherence of the novel, have children.[36]

Conversely, the non-problematic community of the revolutionary combatants in *Le Temps du Mépris* is open to the future and that is why the existence of Kassner's and Anna's child is just as necessary, aesthetically, to this work as was the fact that Kyo and May had no children in *La Condition humaine*.

Like *Les Conquérants, La Condition humaine,* and *Le Temps du Mépris, L'Espoir* constitutes a new stage in Malraux's *oeuvre*, that of the explicit identification with the outlook of the Communist Party as a party opposed to the spontaneous tendencies of the revolutionary community.

Basically, it is the world of *La Condition humaine* seen, not from the point of view of the group of Shanghai revolutionaries, but from that of the Hankow leadership. Furthermore, at the end of the work, Malraux, who is a coherent writer, draws all the consequences from his position, including those that the Stalinist leaders probably envisaged, but refrained from affirming explicitly, and, for the first time in his novels of revolution, denies the absolute, privileged, and unchallengeable character of revolution as the primary and fundamental value.

Indeed, having throughout the book attributed to discipline a primordial value in the name of efficacity and victory, having justified on the basis of this conception the sacrifice of all the *immediate* values of the authentic revolutionary community, Malraux, in the mouth of the communist Garcia, actually declares that the essential struggle is no longer between the revolution and reaction, humanism and barbarity, or even between nationalism and communism, or nationalism and the proletariat, but between the organized parties of which there are at least two — the Communist Party and the Fascist Party, who each have the conquest of the world at stake:

'At the beginning of the war loyal Falangists died shouting, "Long live Spain!" But later it was "Long live the Falangists!" Are you sure that among your airmen the type of communist who at first died shouting "Long live the Proletariat!" or "Long live Communism!" doesn't shout today, in the same circumstances: "Long live the Party!" '

'They won't have much more shouting to do, anyway, for they are nearly all either in hospital or under the ground. Perhaps it's all a matter of personal feelings. Atteignies would probably shout: "Long live the Party!", the others, something else.'

'The word "Party" is misleading, in any case. It is most difficult to group together under one label a mass of people united because they voted the same way, and parties whose ultimate roots strike down into the deep, irrational bedrock of human nature. The age of Parties is beginning, my friend.'. . .

'Don't let us exaggerate out victory. This battle is no Battle of the Marne. But it's victory, all the same. There were more unemployed here than Blackshirts, that's why I arranged for the propaganda by loudspeakers, which you will remember. Still, we were fighting actual fascist units. We should regard this patch of ground with due deference, my friend, for it is our Valmy. The two real parties have come up against each other here for the first time.'[37]

Of course, we should neither overestimate nor underestimate the importance of this passage; *L'Espoir* is based entirely on *the difference of nature* between the 'two true parties', between a barbarous fascism that defends the interests of the privileged few and revolutionary communism that struggles for the triumph of human dignity and universal fraternity. However, by stressing, throughout the book, the primordial character of discipline in relation to all other values, Malraux finally glimpses at the end of the work, at the moment when, as he himself says, 'the war enters a new phase', the extreme consequences of this point of view.

I would even go so far as to say that the relation between the passage quoted above and *L'Espoir* as a whole is analogous, though in an inverse way, with the relation already encountered between the isolated phrase on love in *La Voie royale* and the world of the novel, which ignores and excludes the existence of love. In each case, there are elements that do not form part of the world of the novel, but which are situated in an extension of this world's lines of force at a level at which it would be superseded – in the direction of human community and freedom on the one hand and, on the other, of rigid discipline and barbarity.

But let us return to *L'Espoir*. Of all Malraux's novels it is the longest and the most difficult to analyse on account of the simplicity and poverty of structure of its world. Whether intended or not, Malraux the writer must have been aware of this simplicity and poverty, for instead of a coherent narrative of the kind to be found in his earlier works he has given us a large number of isolated and partial scenes the repetition of which might have been continued indefinitely.

For this very reason it is difficult to remember the characters in the narrative. There are really no individual characters, only groups of characters within which the individuals resemble one another and can be mistaken for one another. That is to say, each of them is merely a fraction of an abstract collective character, the most important of them being the courageous and undisciplined *anarchists*; the *Catholics*, efficient, disciplined, but handicapped by scruples of conscience; and the *communists*, consciously disciplined and highly efficient to the extent that they regard as of secondary importance all considerations that might impede efficiency. Beside these three main archetypes, there are other less important groups – the artists, the mercenaries, the people, etc.

Now the three schematic types I have just indicated correspond strictly to the stereotyped image that the Communist Party has tried to give of the Spanish revolution – an image which, though it contained a certain truth, was to say the least extremely partial.

However valid this point of view may or may not have been, it has two consequences for the world of the narrative: an extremely important one and a more incidental one.

The first is that the political dimension of the conflicts is eluded, the conflicts being transposed entirely on to the military plane whereas, in *La Condition humaine*, on the contrary, they were seen in all their complexity.

Let us deal simply with the opposition between the anarchists (to which we should add the P.O.U.M. (Partido Obrero de Unificación Marxista), which Malraux hardly mentions) and the communists. In reality, what was at issue was not only, of course a problem of discipline, but also of two conceptions of revolutionary strategy, the same that, in *La Condition humaine*, opposed the Shanghai group to the Hankow leadership.

Should the revolution be pushed forward, distributing land to the peasants, handing over the management of the factories to workers' councils and, therefore, gathering against oneself all the anti-socialist forces against which one would throw only the union of national and international revolutionary forces, or would it be better to confine oneself, in China, to the struggle against imperialism and, in Spain, to the struggle against fascism, in the hope of preserving the alliance between communists and bourgeois democrats (nationalists in China, republicans in Spain), the alliance between the proletariat and the democratic or nationalist bourgeoisie?

On this point, there was a radical antagonism between, on the one hand, the non-communist Left and, on the other, the Stalinist leadership. But whichever position one took up, it is obvious that it was both a political and military problem, knowledge of which the non-communist Left tried to blur and whose real aspect the communist leadership tried to hide by shifting it in its entirety on to the level of military discussion, in the case of the anarchists, and on to the level of sabotage and treason in the case of the communist opposition. It is in this sense that *La Condition humaine*, which threw light on the over-all political and military implications of the divergence, was, by doing just that, a pro-Trotskyist book (though Malraux himself tended rather to the positions of the Communist Party leadership). *L'Espoir*, on the other hand, illuminates the political aspects almost entirely by placing it on the level of discipline and organization. As such, it is a book written from a Stalinist point of view.

Thus, although it is in this work that one finds, in the mouth of the Communist Garcia, the phrase later to become famous, to the effect that the best that a man can do in life is to convert 'as wide a range of

experience as possible into conscious thought,' (1968b:338) the values
of the book are strictly opposed to him since, a dozen lines earlier the
same Garcia tells us that for the intellectual:

> . . . the political leader cannot but be regarded by the intellectual as
> an impostor, since he preaches a solution of life's problems, without
> telling us what those problems really are. (1968b:337)

Moreover, the work is orientated in its entirety towards the valorization
of leadership and the leader, the central thread being the transformation
of Manuel, an enthusiastic and spontaneous revolutionary, into a
political leader.[38]

Indeed, the few passages in which political problems are discussed
seem to us today to be surprising to say the least. There is, it is true, the
one in which the intellectual Alvear defends fundamental human values
against the necessities of action. But Alvear is a secondary character and
such a passage is outweighed by the attacks against intellectuals and the
adoption of positions in favour of Stalin:

> 'Intellectuals are always rather inclined to think that a party means a
> collection of people rallied round an idea. A party is really much
> more like a living, acting personality than an abstraction . . .
>
>   The great intellectual is a man of subtleties, of fine shades, of
> evaluations; he's interested in absolute truth and in the complexity
> of things. He is – how shall I put it? – "antiManichean" by
> definition, by nature. But all forms of action are Manichean, because
> all action pays a tribute to the devil; that Manichean element is most
> intense when the masses are involved. Every true revolutionary is a
> born Manichean. The same is true of politics, all politics.'. . .
>
>   'Remember this, Scali: in all countries, in all parties, the
> intellectuals are always at loggerheads. Adler against Freud, Sorel
> against Marx. But in politics a dissenter is an outlaw. The
> intelligentsia always has a tremendous sympathy for the outlaw; out
> of generosity, or because they appreciate his cleverness. But they
> forget that what a party wants is to make good, not to find good
> reasons for its programme.'
>
>   'I grant you that those who, on humane or intellectual grounds,
> may feel inclined to pick holes in revolutionary politics, know
> nothing of the stuff of which a revolution's made. And the men with
> practical experience of revolutions never have the talent of
> Unamuno; often they are incapable of expressing themselves at all.'
>
>   'If, for instance, as we are always being told, there are too many
> pictures of Stalin in Russia, it's not because that ogre Stalin,

squatting in a corner of the Kremlin, has decreed it should be so. Why, look at the craze for signs and badges right here in Madrid, and, heaven knows, the Government doesn't care a damn one way or the other! It would be interesting to analyse the reasons for all those portraits. The trouble is, to talk about love to a lover, you've got to have been in love yourself; it's not enough just to have dissected love in the laboratory. It isn't by approving something or resenting it that a thinker proves his worth, but by his power of exposition. Let the intellectual first explain why and how things are as they are; then he can lodge his protests if he thinks fit — only, by then, it'll be a waste of breath . . . Analysis is a great force, Scali. I don't believe in ethical systems which exclude psychology.' (1968b:334–6)

Finally, I should like to quote one of the few passages that touch on the political aspect of the conflict between anarchists and communists, and which goes very far in the consequences it draws from the point of view from which the work is written. It occurs in a discussion between the communist Garcia and the Christian revolutionary Hernandez in which the latter describes the difficulties he experiences in his relations with the communists, though he is, on the essential points, politically in agreement with them. Since he is a Christian, these scruples are primarily of a moral order:

'Last week one of my men — a "comrade" of sorts, who is or sets up to be an anarchist — was accused of having rifled the company cash-chest. He cited me as a witness. I gave evidence in his favour. But it seems that this man has been imposing the collective system on a village which was in his charge, and his mates were beginning to extend that system to neighbouring villages. I quite agree that the whole idea was a bad one, that it's infuriating for a peasant who needs a sickle to have to sign a dozen forms before he gets one. I admit, too, that the communist method of dealing with such matters is the best.'

'But ever since I gave that evidence, they have their knife into me. It can't be helped — damn it, I'm not going to have a man who cites me as his witness, and whom I know to be innocent, labelled a thief.'

'The communists — and all who want to get things going properly just now — consider that the fact your friend's an innocent man doesn't prevent him from playing into Franco's hands, if what he does leads to unrest amongst the peasants. The communists, you see, *want to get things done*. Whereas you and the anarchists, for different reasons, want to *be* something. That's the tragedy of a revolution like this one. Our respective ideals are so different:

pacifism and the need to fight in self-defence; organization and
Christian sentiment; efficiency and justice – nothing but
contradictions. We've got to straighten them out, transform our
Apocalyptic vision into an army – or be exterminated. That's all.'
(1968b:181–2)

On the basis of what I have just said, pages and pages could be filled
with quotations reaffirming the fundamental themes of the work: the
courage, lack of organization and discipline of the anarchists; the sense
of responsibility, efficiency, and discipline of the communists; the
moral difficulties of the Catholics, which they nevertheless overcome
under the influence of the lessons learnt from the reality of the
struggle; the danger of mixing sentiment and morality with political and
military considerations; the repeated affirmation that every crisis is, in
the final resort, a crisis of leadership; the need for organization and
discipline; the existence of a virile fraternity among the combatants.

We must, of course, limit ourselves to a few examples. Let us begin
with a comparison between the anarchists and the communists:

For the first time, Puig had an impression that he was witnessing,
not a hopeless struggle like that of '34 – like every other he had seen
so far – but quite possibly a victory in the making. Though he had
studied Bakunin – perhaps he was the only member of the group
who had read that author between the lines – he had always looked
on the Spanish revolution as another *Jacquerie*. Since he saw no
hope for the world, exemplary revolts were the utmost he could
hope from anarchism. And so for him every political crisis resolved
itself into a test of character and courage. (1968b:23)

In a conversation with Ximenez, Puig remarks that the attack had
been a good one: ' "Yes. Your men are good in a scrap, but they're no
soldiers." ' (1968b:26)

Or again, in a conversation between Manuel and Ramos:

'I've just been having the hell of a hoo-ha with our men,' said
Ramos. 'Half an hour ago! Ten of them wanted to go home to
dinner; one man actually wanted to trot back to Madrid!'
    'It's the hunting season now; they can't tell the difference. And
how did your "hoo-ha" pan out?'
    'Five are staying, seven leaving. If they were communists, every
man would stay.' (1968b:73–4)

Or between Hernandez and Garcia:

'What do you think of this barricade?' Garcia watched his
companion from the corner of an eye.

'I think as you do. And now I'm going to show you
something . . .'

Hernandez went up to the man apparently in charge of the
barricade. He had the jovial face of an old-time cabby, a
swashbuckling moustache, and knock-out Mexican hat, and was
lavishly tattooed. Strapped to his left arm was a death's head in
aluminium.

'You should raise that barricade eighteen inches, spread out your
men, and post some at the windows on both flanks.'

'Py . . . pers,' growled the 'Mexican' amid a series of detonations
fairly close at hand.

'What?'

'Yer pypers, blast you, yer id-entity pypers!'

'I'm Captain Hernandez in charge of the Zocodover sector.'

'Then you don't belong to the C.N.T., and my barricade ain't
none of your bloody business. See?' (1968:107)

A traitor is discovered:

'I've sent three mates to settle his hash.'

'I'd cashiered him once, damn it! If the F.A.I. hadn't gone and
reinstated him . . .' (1968b:103)

Garcia is speaking to Magnin:

'For me, Monsieur Magnin, the whole problem consists in this: a
popular movement, or a revolution, or even a rebellion, can hold on
to its victory only by methods directly opposed to those which gave
it victory. Sometimes opposed even to the sentiments from which it
started out. Just think it over – in the light of your own experience.
For I doubt if you expect to keep your Flight up to the mark on a
basis of mere fraternity.

The apocalyptic mood clamours for everything right away.
Tenacity of purpose wins through bit by bit; slowly, laboriously.
That apocalyptic fervour is ingrained in every one of us; and there's
the danger. For that fervour spells certain defeat, after a relatively
short period, and for a very simple reason: it's in the very nature of
an apocalypse to have no future . . . Even when it professes to have
one.'

Putting his pipe back in his pocket, he added sadly: 'Our humble
task, Monsieur Magnin, is to *organize* the apocalypse.' (1968b:102)

And later, Enrique says:

The communists are disciplined already. They obey their group
secretaries and military delegates (often, you know, the same men

hold both posts). Any number of people who want to take part in the war joined the Party, just because it's decently organized, and that appeals to them. Formerly our lot were disciplined because they were communists; now plenty of people become communists because the Party stands for discipline. (1968b:68)

In another place Sembrano asks:

'How do you think they managed it in Russia?'. . .
    '*They* had rifles. *Plus* four years' discipline and active service. And the communists, as you know, stood for discipline.' (1968:68)

On the importance of leadership we have Ximenez: ' "It's a sheer waste of time discussing their shortcomings. Once an army has to take the field, something wrong with the troops always means something wrong with the staff-work." ' (1968b:146)
    Heinrich: ' "In such cases . . . it's always the staff-work that's at fault." ' (1968b:207)
    Manuel: 'They bolted because they weren't officered. Before that, they fought as well as we did.' (1968b:226)
    The episodes whose frequent presence constitutes the principal beauty of the book are those that stress the courage of the combatants and the virile fraternity that binds them to each other and to the people. Whatever reservations one might have as to the literary value of the whole work, there are a number of scenes that one probably never forgets once one has read them; for example, the descent of the wounded airmen down the mountain; the attack on the Alcazar; the emotions of the peasant who is asked to identify his village and who, from the height of the plane, can no longer recognize it, etc. To make this observation, however, is also to observe that Malraux, who is a very great writer, has, deliberately or not, compensated for the impossibility of a dense, structured narrative with this series of sketches, which, though moving and marvellously written, follow one another without even forming a true montage.
    Let us return however to some of the elements of the narrative that strike me as being particularly important and characteristic.
    The skeleton of the book, which is fairly vaguely drawn, and which tends to become dissolved in the mass of episodes, is the double passage:

a) from the anarchistic Spanish revolution to organization, from the apocalypse to discipline, from the guerilla to the army;

b) from the character of Manuel, from the sentimental revolutionary, full of love and enthusiasm, to the conscious Communist who masters his feelings, to the military leader.

For the revolutionary forces, this passage involves an increasingly strict and rigid organization, and, for Manuel, who becomes one of the leaders of this organization, a gradual moving away from the men and increasing isolation.

Let us take Manuel at four points in the narrative.

In the course of a conversation Ximenez says to him:

'Soon,' he said 'you'll have to start training young officers. They want to be beloved. That's only human. And it's an excellent thing, my boy, provided you get them to grasp this: an officer should be liked for the way he uses his authority – because he's more competent, just, better than the average – not for his personal charm. Do you see what I mean when I say an officer ought never to "play up" to his men?'. . .

'Yes, it's a most dangerous foible, wanting to be loved. . . . It takes more nobility to be a leader of men, . . . than to be oneself; and it's far harder . . . .' (1968b:148)

As he leaves the court-martial, which has condemned the deserters to death, two of the condemned young men cling to his knees, begging for mercy:

'They've no call to shoot us!' one of the men was shouting. 'We're volunteers! You got to tell them!' . . .

'They can't do it! They can't do it!' the other began to shout. 'They can't sir!'. . .

Manuel felt inclined to say: 'The court-martial's nothing to do with me.' But he was ashamed of such a disavowal . . .

Manuel wondered what he could say to them. The argument for their defence was something inexpressible in words; it was in that streaming face, that open mouth, which had made Manuel aware that here was the everlasting visage of the man who pays. Never had he realized so keenly the necessity of choosing between victory and compassion. (1968b:331–2)

Later, when recounting the same scene to Ximenez, he says:

I knew what had to be done, and I did it. I'm determined to serve my party, and I'm not going to let myself be deterred by any personal psychological reactions. I don't believe in regrets. But there's something else . . . I take upon myself responsibility for those executions. They were necessary to save the lives of others . . . our men's. But there's something else; every step I've taken towards greater efficiency, towards becoming a better officer, has estranged me more and more from my fellow-men. Every day I'm getting a little less human. (1968b:347–8)

Finally at the moment the book concludes:

Last spasmodic bursts of gunfire were rumbling in the distance. His lines established, Manuel, followed by his dog, was going round the village to get hold of some lorries. He had adopted a magnificent — ex-fascist —Alsatian dog, and it had been wounded four times. The more he felt cut off from men, the more he loved animals: bulls, army horses, large dogs and fighting cocks. (1968b:426)

The nature of this education undergone by Manuel, the revolutionary combatants, and the Spanish people through the reality of the struggle emerges clearly: all that is immediately and spontaneously human must be relegated and even abolished in the name of an exclusive concern for efficiency. The essential theme of *L'Espoir* is formulated in a few lines by Garcia:

There are just wars, such as the one we're waging now — but there's no such thing as a just army. And that an intellectual, a man who's business it is to think, should go and say like Miguel: 'I'm leaving you because you are not just' — well, it strikes me, my friend, as downright immoral. Yes, one can have a policy that's just, but there's no such thing as a just party. (1968b:339)

And he may well be right, but perhaps only in part, for, between the impotent morality that Malraux always seems to be attributing to the Catholics and anarchists, and subordination of the means to the end, which has always been the doctrine of the theoreticians of the State, from Machiavelli to Stalin, there is a third position that sees in the means/ends relation a totality in which the end acts upon the means and conversely.

But it is not our task here to discuss the validity of Malraux's point of view — this would be quite out of place in the context of a literary critical study. Our task is simply to show that the very structure of this point of view entirely eliminates one of the important dimensions of the reality described in the work.

To conclude this analysis, which is even more schematic — and this says a great deal, I readily admit — than those of Malraux's other works, I should like to stress once more two characteristics of the novel which, I think, derive from this same structure.

Firstly, as in all Malraux's other works, there is a strict coherence between the over-all vision and the private lives of the characters. That is why, with man reduced to disciplined combat and military organization, there is no longer any place for erotic or amorous relationships of any kind between men and women.

L'Espoir is a book of combat in which one no longer finds either love, eroticism, family, or, to be more precise, in which these elements are present only as obstacles to the values of the work.

'War makes one chaste,' Manuel says on one occasion, and apart from the episode in which a letter is sent to the wife of the commander of the Alcazar, the scene of the militia-woman bringing meals to the combatants, and a reference to Caballero's son, who has been taken prisoner by the fascists in Segovia and who will be shot, all the passages concerning women or family simply indicate that their presence would be detrimental, not to say fatal, to the combatants.

There is, for example, the particularly characteristic passage in which a woman wants to remain with her husband:

'Do you think I ought to leave?'

'She's a German comrade,' Guernico explained to Garcia, but did not answer her.

'He says I ought to go,' the woman went on. 'He says he can't fight properly when I'm near.'

'And I'm quite sure he's right,' Garcia said.

'But I just can't *live* if I know he's fighting here and I don't even hear what's happening.'. . .

The women are all alike, Garcia mused. If that one goes, she'll take it hard ar first, but she'll see it through; whereas, if she stays, he'll be killed . . .

'Why do you want to stay?' Guernico's voice was gentle.

'I don't mind dying, but food's the trouble; I got to eat my fill, and now that won't be possible . . . I'm in the family way.'
(1968b:263)

And later, when Garcia and Guernico are left alone: 'What's hardest,' Guernico continued in a low tone, 'is the problem of the wives and children. Anyhow I've that much luck, my family's not here.'
(1968b:270)

Or again when Manuel is recounting to Ximenez the scene of this deserter:

Last week I slept with a woman whom I'd loved in vain . . . for years. Well, after two wretched shots at it, I found myself wanting to get away. No, I haven't any regrets on that score. But if I give up all that, it must be for some good reason. To command is to serve, nothing more and nothing less. (1968b:347)

Secondly, the fact should be noted that *L'Espoir* describes not the defeat of the revolution, but victory after a battle, and that, in the context of the story, this victory suggests that of the Spanish revolution.

Of course, there could be a very simple explanation for this, namely that Malraux, who published the novel in 1937, before the end of the war, did not wish to make the slightest alteration to an already published work.

I admit that this is a very plausible hypothesis. But it may also be — and I think that it is worth mentioning it — that this refusal to take later events into account derives from an internal necessity of the work's structure: the world of the book is centred on the duty to sacrifice to discipline, in the name of efficiency, all other values, and therefore this sacrifice would seem unjustified and derisory if, far from being effective, it culminated not in victory, but in defeat.

This may be why the last very short paragraphs with which the book ends open up on to a vision of peace and even of a future in which war no longer exists. During the fighting, Manuel had given up music, women, and any kind of personal pleasure. He had once said to Gartner that he was separated from music; he now realizes that what he most wishes at that moment, alone in a street of a conquered city, is to hear music.

But what he hears is not the *Internationale* or any other battle song, but Beethoven's symphonies and the *Adieux* sonata:

He felt the seething life around him charged with portents, as though some blind destiny lay in wait for him behind those lowering cloudbanks which the guns no longer racked. The Alsatian was listening, lying full length like the dogs in bas-reliefs. Some day there would be peace. And he, Manuel, would become another man, someone he could not visualize as yet; just as the soldier he had become could no more visualize the Manuel who once bought a little 'bus' to go ski-ing in the Sierra.

Most likely it was the same with all those others moving through the streets, and the same with the men he could hear strumming their favourite tunes on pianos open to the public gaze — the men whose heavy pointed cowls had led the battle yesterday . . . But war may be discovered only once in a lifetime; life, many times.

As the strands of melody took form, interwoven with his past, they conveyed to him the self-same message that the dim sky, those ageless fields, and that town which had stopped the Moors might, too, have given him. For the first time Manuel was hearing the voice of that which is more awe-inspiring even than the blood of men, more enigmatic even than their presence on the earth — the infinite possibilities of their destiny. And he felt that this new consciousness within him was linked up with the sounds of running water in the street and the footfalls of the prisoners, profound and permanent as the beating of his heart. (1968b:437–8)

Like *Le Temps du Mépris, L'Espoir* is a book that approaches the epic, but which doesn't seem to me to have reached it either, though for essentially different, not to say opposed, reasons. In *Le Temps du Mépris,* the supersession of the individual was a problem and even if one showed that the problem was soluble, that the supersession could be achieved, the very presence of the individual and the supersession created a pre-epic world. As Malraux himself said, the book ended at a moment when 'a god had just been born', whereas the epic, which poses no problems and knows no individuals separated from the community, specifically presupposes the real, unchallenged and non-problematic presence of the gods.

L'Espoir appears, conversely, as a world that might be termed 'post-epic' in so far as the individual, instead of realizing himself in the community and forming with it an organic unity, finds himself denied spontaneity and plenitude by discipline and organization. Basically, with these two works, whose world is centred on the reconciliation of the individual and the collectivity, Malraux passed from the stage preceding this reconciliation to a stage at which he made political and military technocracy the true subject of history. For the sociologist, however, the problem posed by this passage is not so much that of Malraux's personal development as that of deciding whether at the period at which the two works were written, we are dealing with a more general process. Once again we have to remember that the writer does not develop abstract ideas, but creates an imaginary reality and that the possibilities of this creation do not depend primarily on his intentions but on the social reality in which he lives and the mental frameworks that he has helped to elaborate. So, in order to answer the question posed, the first thing to do would no doubt be to examine French literature of the Inter-War period in order to see how many sufficiently important works succeeded in describing a world centred on the value of revolutionary spontaneity, or at least on the unity of man and the community, rather than works centred on the value of discipline and efficiency.

Meanwhile, to complete this study, all that remains is to analyse *Les Noyers de l'Altenburg*, which appeared in 1943 and is Malraux's last fictional work. At first sight it is a rather curious book, since one senses while reading it the existence of a fairly strict and rigorous internal unity, whereas it is presented as a series of isolated scenes, situated at different times, with at least two different heroes, the connection between whom is far from clear. In fact, I shall try to show that the unity of the text becomes visible if one takes into account that it belongs to a particular literary genre that is much closer to the essay than to fictional literature or the epic.

What is an essay? In principle, as Lukács has shown in a famous study, it is an autonomous literary form situated midway between philosophy, a conceptual expression of a world-view, and literature, the imaginary creation of a world of individual persons and concrete situations. Between the two, the essay is an intermediate genre in so far as it poses *conceptual problems* (and the great essays in the history of literature tend to pose problems rather than provide answers) *in terms of a particular concrete situation* or *individual character*. That is why the essay has always an ironical dimension, since it seems to be dealing with the life or the ideas of a particular character, or recounts how particular events occurred, whereas in reality characters and events are merely the *occasion* that allows the essayist to raise a number of problems of universal value. It should be added that the form of the essay is very often, from the historical and even biographical point of view, a transitional form that the author adopts precisely because neither the questions nor the answers are yet sufficiently mature to be expressed in a directly conceptual form.

Having said this, it seems to me that *Les Noyers de l'Altenburg* is very close in form to the essay, without however being an essay in the strict sense of the term. In common with the essay, it has the double dimension, it too poses *conceptual problems in terms of* a series of *individual and concrete realities*. But it differs from the essay because instead of taking these individual characters or concrete situations from a present or past reality as many of the great essayists have done or from literature itself as most of them have done, Malraux, who is a writer, has himself imagined, in a series of episodes, the concrete situations through which he has raised the problems he wished to discuss with his readers. It also differs from the essay in that it is not content to raise problems, but provides a fairly complex reply, which deprives it of the ironical dimension and replaces, on the level of ideas, the spontaneous irony proper to most essays with the development of a more or less coherent demonstration. If one reads the book from this point of view, the different episodes present a rigorous and irreversible order in the exposition of its true subject, Malraux's new conception of man and the reasons that led him to abandon the Communist movement and ideology.

Is this evolution in Malraux an individual phenomenon or, on the contrary, a fact bound up with the sociopolitical events of the period, and, as such, with the ideological currents that manifested themselves in the collective consciousness or at least in intellectual circles? As always when we have raised problems of this kind, the reply could only emerge from an enormous study in depth of all the documents of the period and, since this research has not been carried out, we can do no more, of course, than stress the need to undertake such research. Nevertheless, it might be said that, quite obviously, the German-Soviet Non-Aggression Pact of 1939, though perfectly comprehensible from the point of view of the USSR's anti-capitalist (and therefore, too, anti-Nazi) foreign policy, had caused a crisis in the conscience of a great many Western socialist intellectuals. It showed clearly a much deeper reality than most of them were aware of — the fact that belonging to the Communist movement demanded during the Stalinist period, or at least could demand, a choice between the immediate interests of the Soviet State considered as the principal conquest of socialism and the immediate interests of the society and proletariat of the country in which they lived.

Malraux had no doubt already described this problem in Chinese terms in *La Condition humaine* and, at the time, although his novel brought out the poignant and tragic side of the situation, he nevertheless ended the work with the affirmation that:

> Work must become the chief weapon of class-warfare. The most tremendous industrialization plan in the world is at present under consideration. Its object is in the course of five years to transform the entire USSR and make it a leading industrial power in Europe; next to overtake and surpass the United States. (1968a:278)

and by the hope that historical development will integrate the struggle and the sacrifice of the Shanghai revolutionaries into the totality of the struggle for socialism.

In 1939, a no doubt different problem presented itself in his own society, in his own country. What was at issue now was not the revolutionary struggle, but military alliances and strategy in international politics. Nevertheless, the two situations were analogous in their fundamental schemata — the need to choose between the immediate interests of the USSR and the immediate interests of

Western society and the Western proletariats. We know that this
problem caused a serious crisis among left-wing intellectuals in
France – though it is, of course, impossible to determine the extent of
its effects. For most of them, this crisis was overcome shortly
afterwards when conflict broke out between Germany and the USSR,
the latter coming in on the side of the Allies. Once again, the politically
strategic character of the Pact and the profoundly anti-Nazi character
of Communist tactics and of Soviet foreign policy became clear.
Nevertheless, the world-wide crisis provoked by the German-Soviet Pact
could have been an important factor in Malraux's change of perspective
and a study of sociological ambitions ought to mention this possibility.

However, let us return to the narrative, the first episode of which
takes place in June 1940 after the defeat of France; several thousand
prisoners are first herded into Chartres Cathedral, then into a public
works yard. In this exceptional situation, old preoccupations and
activities reappear: the building of dug-outs, the search for the last tin
of food, rummaging for the last crumbs at the bottoms of one's
pockets, the walk to the barbed-wire fence to catch a piece of bread
that a woman secretly brings every day to the prisoners.

At one point, in the cathedral, cards are handed out that the
prisoners can send to their families; some of the prisoners write longer
letters; they are warned that they will not be sent. Shortly afterwards,
in the yard, sheets of paper are thrown to the wind – they are the
letters that the prisoners had just written and which the German
administration had ordered to be scattered in this way.

A few moments later the narrator meets a tank-corps man who had
started to write again:

'Are you keeping a diary?'
   He looks up in a daze:
   'A diary?'
   Presently he understands:
   'No ... I ... that sort of thing ...'
   And, as if he were stating the obvious:
   'I'm writing to my wife.'[39]

A little later, when speaking to another prisoner:

'I'm waiting for it to wear off, myself.'
   'What?'
   'Everything. I'm waiting for it to wear off.' (1952:21)

While recounting these facts, Malraux explicitly develops his new
view of man. Fundamental to Marxist thinking and also to Malraux's

previous works was the conviction that all men tend naturally to give a meaning to their lives and by that very fact affirm their dignity. Oppression, economic and social conditions may crush and annihilate in them this natural tendency to action and dignity, but through oppressive structures, which are continually changing throughout history, there remains the sole permanent human reality, the human condition that is the aspiration to dignity and meaning.

Thus, from this point of view, the revolutionaries, both intellectuals and men of action, strive to help men to become aware of the natural aspirations buried within them — aspirations deformed by an oppressive civilization — by bringing them back to what is their true vocation — *action* through the creation of the community and therefore of history. Now it is precisely this view that is brought into question by the first episode of *Les Noyers de l'Altenburg.*

There exists, in effect, not a *fundamental man,* but an *eternal man*; the work says this constantly:

> In this Babylonian hovel, made of pillar-stumps, drain-pipes and branches, there are now three of them writing on their knees, crouched like Peruvian mummies . . . This man has one of those Gothic faces that are more and more numerous now that beards are being grown. The age-old memory of the scourge. The scourge had to come, and here it is. I remember the silent conscripts of September marching through the white dust of the roads and the dahlias of late summer, who seemed to be marching against flood, against fire; but peeping out from underneath that age-old ingenuity, man's secret faith in endurance, however cluttered with disasters, the same faith perhaps as the cave-man used to have in the face of famine. (1952:20—21)

The presence of the prisoners in Chartres Cathedral also had symbolic value:

> In the earlier days of the war, as soon as his uniform had blotted out a man's profession, I began to see these Gothic faces. And what now emerges from the wild crowd that can no longer shave is not the penal settlement, but the Middle Ages . . . Every morning I watch thousands of shadows in the restless light of dawn, and I think; 'It's mankind.' (1952:22—3)

But this man no longer creates gods, values; he is, on the contrary — he who for thousands of years has been living in a 'half-sleep' — an existence that does not change and which, in the face of history, has only one reaction, to submit to it, to find a means of existing through

and despite it and, when this becomes difficult, to oppose to its
anti-human, grandiose and barbarous creations his own cunning, his
age-old and corrosive patience, which always in the end manages to
wear them down. Eternal man, the same through the ages, the same
through meaningful and changing history; mankind and the
'intellectuals'; these are different and often opposed realities:

> I thought I knew more than I had learnt because I had found in one
> faith the two conflicting elements, religious and political; I now
> know that an intellectual is not only a man to whom books are
> necessary, he is any man whose reasoning, however elementary it
> may be, affects and directs his life. These men I am with, these very
> men have been living from day to day for thousands and thousands
> of years. (1952:22–3)

So for the intellectual who speaks through this narrative and who
now knows that action is not the actualization of a potential, but
always effective, community between himself and mankind, and that
the revolutionary ideology was therefore largely mistaken, new
problems arrive that have to be faced. They concern both those who
'have been living from day to day for thousands and thousands of years'
and the man for whom an idea 'affects and directs his life'. (1952:23)
They concern above all their mutual relations:

> Those encounters the tireless wind blows back to me, as it blows
> back at random my comrades' letters. So let me examine them, let
> me compare them with my own, while the pink earth-worms
> summoned by the evening dew creep out once more from the
> ground stamped hard by the feet of five thousand men — while life
> goes on until my enquiries mingle with his in the last fellowship of
> death.
>   In this place, writing is the only way to keep alive. (1952:24)

The narrator confronts these problems through the experience of his
father.

The first episode posed the theoretical problem; the next two
describe in a scarcely transposed way the historical situation, the forces
opposing one another, and the experience that led Malraux to move
away from the revolutionary movement.

The first concerns the nonconformist opposition, for whom one
feels respect and affection, but which committed suicide leaving only
an ambiguous and therefore useless message, and as executors the
intellectuals and men of action who must sort out the inheritance
alone. The second concerns Stalinism.

Having returned to Europe the narrator's father, Victor Berger, is reunited with his own father who, a few days later, commits suicide. He had been an essentially nonconformist individual. When mayor of his commune, he had, in face of the insurmountable hostility of the village and his municipality, given shelter on his own land to a synagogue and to travelling circuses.

A believing Catholic, he was shocked by certain relaxations in the Church's discipline. When he protested about these to his parish priest, he received a dusty answer: 'But Mr Berger, is it proper for a mere priest to question the decisions of Rome?' (1952:30)

So he went to Rome to protest, to express his reservations:

He had made the pilgrimage on foot. As chairman of various good works, he had had no difficulty in obtaining an audience with the Pope. He had found himself with about twenty of the faith in a room in the Vatican. He was not bashful, but the Pope was the Pope, and he was a Christian; they had all knelt down, the Holy Father had walked by, they had kissed his slipper and had been dismissed . . .

On his return, his Protestant friends believed he was ripe for conversion.

'One does not change one's religion at my age.'

Thereafter, cut off from the Church but not from Christ, he attended mass every Sunday outside the building, standing in the midst of the nettles in one of the angles formed by the junction of the nave and the transept, following the service from memory, carefully listening at the window for the shrill sound of the handbell proclaiming the Elevation. (1952:30–31)

In the end, he killed himself, calmly, firmly, accepting his destiny. His first conversations with his son had taken up again the prayer of the Tartar caravaneers from *Le Temps du Mépris*:

'If you could choose another life, what sort would you choose?' 'What sort would you?' He thought it over for quite a time and suddenly said, quite seriously: 'Well, you know, *whatever happens*, if I had to live another life again, I should want none other than Dietrich Berger's.' (1952:64–5)

Like the members of the opposition within the Party, he left an ambiguous will as far as the Church was concerned:

I believe what he went through was extremely painful. You know the will was sealed. The words; 'My express wish is to have a religious burial' were written on a loose sheet placed on the table where the strychnine was; but what he had written first was: 'My express wish is not to have a religious burial.' It was only afterwards he crossed out the negative and scribbled over it several times. He probably didn't have enough strength left to tear the paper up and begin again. (1952:66–7)

He is quite explicit as to the narrator's view of suicide:

'I have heard a lot of nonsense talked about suicide,' my father used to say, 'but for a man who kills himself boldly I have never encountered any feeling but respect. Whether suicide is an act of courage or not is a question which concerns only those who have not killed themselves.' (1952:28)

As I have already said, the third episode poses, in terms of Victor Berger's action, the problem of official communism; the transposition is scarcely concealed.

An orientalist, a professor at the University of Constantinople, and a German officer,[40] Victor Berger is led to act in Turkey, partly with the agreement of the German embassy's secret service, partly independently and against these services.

A multi-national state, threatened with dislocation, Turkey is ruled by Sultan Abdul-Hamid. The Sultan's entire policy is directed to the possibility of developing pan-Islamism, which seems to him capable of constituting the only counterpoise to the forces of dislocation. Victor Berger is hostile to the Sultan and makes contact with the Young Turk opposition, with whom he believes the future of Turkey lies, and gets the German secret services to support them. With German help, he then sets about organizing the propaganda service which, like Garine before him, he turns into a remarkable instrument for action: 'Out of propaganda, a mere device, he was bent on creating a means of political action.' (1952:39)

A first revolution breaks out. Abdul-Hamid is deposed and replaced by Mohammed V; the power of Parliament is definitively established.

The German secret services refuse to go further or to continue their support of Berger, who remains linked with the Young Turks. The movement develops. One day, a special envoy from Bulow asks Victor Berger:

'What are Enver Pasha's intentions . . . his plans?'
　　'To return as soon as possible, and to seize power.'
　　'Although the Government is not exactly strong, I . . .'
　　'We shall seize power.'
At the word 'we' the envoy pricked up his ears. (1952:48)

Victor Berger had, in fact, gone over entirely to the side of Enver Pasha and the Young Turks.

Later, with or without the support of his government (which, indeed, sometimes finds it useful to keep in contact with the Young Turks and even to support them), Victor Berger supports Enver Pasha who seizes power and turns Turkey into a modern state with a well-organized army.

Now Enver also represents a supranational ideology, Ottomanism, and, despite the suspicions of the German embassy, Victor Berger becomes one of the propaganda agents of this ideology throughout Asia. One day, however, he is attacked by a fanatical madman who reproaches him for not being a Turk:

> My father went back to his house in a rage, severed and somehow released from a spell: suddenly, abruptly, he realized the truth: Ottomanism, the incentive to the new Turkish aspirations which had perhaps saved Constantinople, simply did not exist. (1952:54)

If his and Enver's actions had any efficacy it was to the extent that they corresponded to the real interests of certain tribes and could be based on what, in the last resort, had proved in a certain sense to be an effective force: Abdul Hamid's pan-Islamism:

> He now knew what one could expect from these people. They would willingly fight for Enver, the victorious general who had become the Caliph's son-in-law; that is, on condition he paid them well and the risk was not too great (they would have thought twice about fighting against England). In the name of Ottomanism? Certainly. Islam would have been enough. Besides, wherever my father had made his mark, it was thanks to the old pan-Islamic agents of Abdul Hamid. (1952:55)

Behind Enver's Ottomanism lay the interests of the Turkish state. Victor Berger tried, out of loyalty, and without much hope of success, to explain to Enver:

> This discussion seemed pointless. Having been seriously ill at Ghazni, he had contributed to a mistake which had made great demands on himself; but with his health restored his hate returned: as though he had been deceived, not by himself, but by that false, idiotic Central Asia which rejected its own destiny, and by all those who had shared in his belief.
>   'I should have sent a Moslem in the first place,' said Enver. (1952:37)

In all this, there is an obvious transposition of the contemporary situation: for Turkey, of course, we must read Russia, for Abdul Hamid the Tsarist government, for pan-Islamism pan-Slavism, for the first Turkish revolution supported by Germany the February revolution supported by the Western powers, for Ottomanism communism and lastly for Enver Pasha probably Stalin.[41]

Using these episodes, let us pause for a while to examine the figure of Victor Berger, an intellectual who has become a man of action because, according to him, it is the only way to engage and order one's life according to an idea. (In answer to his uncle, who defined man by his secrets, he opposes the brief, laconic phrase: 'Man is what he does'.)

In the conversation mentioned above with Bulow's special envoy, we are told why he committed himself to Ottomanism:

'How is it,' he asked, 'that you feel so . . . so personally interested in Ottomanism? Enthusiastic about it, if I may say so'. . .

'Activity which is fostered by dreams instead of being blighted by them is hard to find,' he said, half in jest. Then, with a broader grin: 'What have you got to offer me that's better?' (1952:49–50)

The first three episodes of the work enabled Malraux to define his new view of man and to show why he had broken with both official communism, which in reality is merely the ideology of one state, and with the opposition, which is no doubt morally respectable, but which had virtually committed suicide. Two particularly important pages describe Victor Berger's return to Marseilles. There he discovers everyday reality, people living from day to day, shop windows, 'the most ordinary things, streets, dogs . . .' (1952:59) But he also discovers that when one has committed oneself to action, one can no longer go back. The words of an anarchist published in a newspaper keep running through his head: 'The identity of the victim is of no importance! But afterwards, something unforeseen happens: everything is different, the most ordinary things, streets, for instance, dogs . . .' (1952:60)

He remembers a great disappointment from his Paris youth: 'This evening he felt released, as he had felt then – with a rapturous liberty which was indistinguishable from license.' (1952:61)

The fourth, and most important, episode in the work is the discussion at Altenburg. This was probably modelled on the literary weekends at Pontigny, in which Malraux often participated. Like Pontigny, Altenburg is a place in which the leading thinkers of Europe meet. Victor Berger is present not only as an intellectual but also as a man of action who has long fascinated intellectuals, whereas in reality he has ceased to be one. The discussion in which he takes part begins when most of the great intellectuals have left, with the exception, that is, of Molberg, an anthropologist, an Africanist, and probably a sort of mixture of Frobenius, Spengler, and Malraux himself, whose great Hegelian synthesis of the philosophy of history is eagerly awaited by the scientific world. In fact, like the narrator himself, Molberg has discovered the break between ideas and eternal man and therefore the impossibility of any philosophy of this kind. So, under the influence of his African experience, he has destroyed what he had already written of his work and hung the leaves 'from the lower branches of various types of tree from the Sahara to Zanzibar'. (1952:82)

The ground is prepared for the discussion in several significant episodes; I shall mention just two.

There is the account of the last journey Walter[42] made with a now insane Nietzsche in order to bring him back to Basle in a third-class railway compartment. As they emerged from a tunnel, Friedrich sang 'a poem which was unknown to us; and it was his latest poem, *Venice*. I don't like Friedrich's compositions. They're mediocre. But this song . . . well, by God, it was sublime.' (1952:72)

Hearing this song, Walter came to feel that certain human works were stronger than death, madness, and the absurdity of life, that they 'can withstand the intoxication provoked by the contemplation of our dead, of the starlit sky, of history'. (1952:73–4)

Victor Berger would be inclined to agree with him, but in his consciousness Nietzsche's song is linked with the face of his grandfather lying dead at Reichbach; for the first time in the book, the central theme, that of the relation between creation and life, appears:

This natural gift that Walter was talking about, how much more effective it was against the starlit sky than against sorrow. And perhaps it could have applied to a certain dead man's face, had that face not been a face he loved. For Walter, man was nothing but the 'wretched pile of secrets' made to foster these works in the deep shadows surrounding his motionless face; for my father, the whole starlit sky was contained in the attitude of mind which caused a man already possessed by the death-wish to say, at the end of a frequently painful, unglamourous life: 'If I had to choose another life, I should choose my own.' (1952:75)

A little later we learn that Molberg had filled his room with tiny clay figures that he himself had modelled and which he called his 'monsters'; they were all 'startlingly sad, like Goya's monsters which seem to remember they were once human . . . Some were benevolent, others malevolent. He used to send them to his friends.' (1952:78)

Of course, these monsters devoid of sense, expressive of a nostalgia for a mankind that they can no longer attain, correspond to the message that now, after destroying his work, Molberg can still transmit.

In describing the discussion, I cannot enter into the details of the conflicting opinions and I must also leave aside the irony that Malraux expressed for certain kinds of intellectual. The central figure is that of Molberg, who, having abandoned a work that was to provide a 'ruthless and perfectly coherent interpretation of man', (1952:81) now develops the Spenglerian thesis of strictly closed, non-communicating civilizations, beneath which there exists no other permanent reality than the rude peasant. For him, cultures are no more than sets of significant forms imposed on a neutral and indifferent material: eternal man is not historical:

> Fundamental man is a myth, an intellectual's dream about peasants: just try to dream about the fundamental workman! Will you have it that for the peasant the world is not made of oblivion? Those who have learnt nothing have nothing to forget. A wise peasant, I know what that is; but it's not fundamental man! There's no such thing as fundamental man, developed, according to the age he lives in, by what he thinks and believes: there is man who thinks and believes, or nothing. A civilization is not an ornament, but a structure. Look! We all know our friend Walter's craze: those two Gothic sculptures and that figurehead are of the same wood, as you know. But those forms are not shaped from fundamental walnut, but from logs of wood. (1952:111)

As for the idea of history, it is simply the form that our culture has tried to impose on this indifferent nature; however, behind history, says Molberg, there may be 'something which is to history what history is to the country, to revolution. Perhaps our consciousness of time — I don't say "our concept" — which is of recent date . . .' (1952:105–6)

The discussion has come to an end. The answer that has emerged from it is, though much fuller and more detailed, the same that Walter had developed in speaking of his journey with Nietzsche: there exists an absurd human reality, devoid of form, on which the creations of intellectuals, cultures, impose temporary meanings, no doubt of a localized kind, but which are man's only hope of giving a provisional meaning to his life and triumphing over nothingness and the absurd.

But as he leaves the hall Victor Berger begins to have the same doubts that he had felt during Walter's conversation about his journey with Nietzsche. He discovers the reality that underlies and justifies these doubts, the reality that the participants in the discussion have forgotten: the walnut trees of Altenburg.

Between the log – wood as raw material – and the Gothic form created by sculpture, there is the living tree that grows and breathes:

He had reached the big trees: fir trees already drowned in darkness, with raindrops still sparkling on the end of every needle; linden trees chattering with sparrows. The loveliest were two walnut trees: he was reminded of the statues in the library . . .

My father was thinking of the two saints, and Atlas. Instead of supporting the weight of the world, the tortured wood of these walnut trees flourished with life everlasting in their polished leaves under the sky and in their nuts that were almost ripe, in all their venerable bulk above the wide circle of young shoots and the dead nuts of winter. 'Civilizations or the animal, like statues or logs . . .' Between the statues and the logs there were the trees, and their design which was as mysterious as that of life itself. And Atlas, and St. Mark's face consumed with Gothic passion, were lost in it like the culture, like the intellect, like everything my father had just been listening to – all buried in the shadow of this kindly statue which the strength of the earth carved for itself, and which the sun at the level of the hills spread across the sufferings of humanity as far as the horizon.

There had been no war in Europe for forty years. (1952:115–6)

With the abandonment of revolutionary ideology, war is the second fundamental reality around which the world of the work is organized. If the episodes recounted in the work are all situated between 1914 and 1940, this may also be to show that it is not about any particular war, but about *war* as such in its relations with mankind and, beyond war itself, about everything that is anti-human and barbarous in the cultures created by intellectuals and men of action.

It is in relation to war that *Les Noyers de l'Altenburg* assumes its full importance.

The intellectuals of Altenburg, the Walters, the Molbergs, had seen only a simplified duality: on the one hand, eternal man living from day to day, the peasant, the formless wood, indifferent and neutral, and, on the other hand, the creation of intellectuals, works of art, cultures.

In fact, permanent man, the man who lives from day to day, Molberg's peasant, was neither indifferent nor neutral. He lived like the walnut trees in the park at Altenburg and if he did not make history, he tried in his everyday life to live, to eat, to clothe himself, to love his fellow men, to have children, and to be happy. That is to say, he was not passive in relation to cultures, but he sifted them for what was favourable to the pursuit of life and happiness, separating it from what was harmful and unhealthy, and if he seldom resisted barbarity actively, he acted nevertheless through his permanence, his age-old patience, which in the end always succeeded in wearing down the institutions and cultures that threatened his nature and aspirations. Having said this, there is no need to spend much time on the last three episodes of the work; though particularly important, their meaning is easy enough to grasp.

Two of these episodes show us what men of action and creative intellectuals can become when their activity is expressed in war and in the encounter between man and life.

Having joined the counter-espionage service, Victor Berger witnesses a scene in which Captain Wurtz tries to use a woman's love for her child, the most intimate, the deepest, most essential aspect of her life, in order to break down a woman he suspects of being a spy. When Wurtz senses Victor Berger's repugnance at such methods, he remarks: 'Methods like these, which you shrink from . . . save the lives of thousands of our soldiers.' (1952:125)

Shortly afterwards, Victor Berger is sent with Captain Wurtz to accompany Professor Hoffman, a remarkable scientist, who has developed an extremely effective new combat gas and who is to organize the first experimental attack against the Russian lines. Wurtz, who is still attached to the ancient values of military courage is repelled by such methods and is given the same answers by Hoffman that he himself had given to Berger:

'If you look at it objectively,' said the Professor in a voice of authority, 'gas constitutes the most humane method of warfare . . .' To the Captain, these two men were enemies. Men of words and figures, 'intellectuals', who wanted to do away with courage. They were belittling it. His own courage was real enough: when taken prisoner by the Russians and condemned to death, he had refused to give the least bit of information, although he was promised a hundred thousand roubles and his freedom in Russia – and had escaped. This fortitude, in his eyes, justified everything, gave him every right. He shook his round, snub-nosed head, as though bothered by invisible flies.

'It'll be a great misfortune,' he said, 'if we're to see the old German method of war vanish from the Empire.'

My father was listening, watching Wurtz turning into a moralist (not to mention the other moralist). In the same way as one watches a madman who looks a bit like oneself. Contrary to my father's views, the Captain had justified the introduction of the child in the name of the soldiers he was saving; and the Professor was repeating

the same argument. We, we, this room was full of saints!
(1952:135–6)

The next episode is the attack itself which, fortunately or
unfortunately, is carried out not only by intellectuals and technicians
such as Wurtz, Hoffman, and Victor Berger, but, on their instructions,
by the mass of soldiers, by those men who live from day to day and
whom Malraux presents to us with their conversations about everyday
life, at dawn, as they await the attack in the trenches.

And when finally the attack is unleashed, we are presented with the
marvellous description of the human reaction, of resistance to
barbarity, of the soldiers who, arriving in the trenches in which they
find thousands of gassed Russians, forget the war and all immediate
reality and feel above all solidarity with their fellow men, with these
victims of the barbarous destiny that civilization has imposed on them.
Ignoring orders to advance, they pick up their gassed enemies and,
returning the way they had come, dash to the ambulances for help.
Victor Berger, puzzled at first, not understanding what is happening,
finally succumbs to the movement and like the others picks up a gassed
Russian and returns behind the lines. On his way, he crosses lorry-loads
of soldiers who look at him in amazement:

> They looked at him with the same uneasiness as men meeting the first
> native in an unknown land; in the same way they would soon be
> looking at the first gas casualty . . . My father also looked at them,
> one after the other: the barrage of pity would not last indefinitely.
> Man can get used to anything, except to dying. (1952:183)

The third part ends with Victor Berger thinking that he himself has
been gassed:

> He was overwhelmed by a lightning-flash of certainty, as urgent as
> this slight hissing in his throat: the aim of life was happiness, and he,
> fool that he was, had been engaged on other things instead of being
> happy! Scruples, human dignity, pity, thought were nothing but a
> monstrous fake, the bird-calls of a sinister power whose mocking
> laughter would ring in one's ears in one's last instant of life. In this
> fierce betrayal and in the clutch of death, there remained only a wild
> hatred of all that had stopped him being happy. He imagined he saw
> the ambulance; he tried to run still faster; his legs thrashed the
> empty air, the whole world suddenly turned upside down, the forest
> hurtled into a sky which was at the same time under his feet.
> (1952:186)

The last episode takes us back to 1940, to the camp at Chartres. The narrator is tormented by one problem: what is man?

I can think only of what holds out against the spell of nothingness. And from wasted day to wasted day I am increasingly obsessed by the mystery which does not conflict with the indeterminate aspect of my companions who sing while they hold out under the infinity of the night sky. Rather does it link it up, by a long-forgotten path, with the nobility which men do not know exists in themselves, with the victorious side to the only animal that knows he has to die. (1952:189–90)

And the book ends with the account of the attack, in which the narrator takes part and during which he finds himself shut up in a tank with three comrades: Bonneau, a pimp, who lives largely in imagination; Léonard, a fireman in a Paris music-hall, who, having once slept with the leading dancer, is constantly living that great moment in his life; Pradé, who was deprived of an education by World War I and who regards the son he hopes to educate as 'all that stands for the absolute in this degrading, gloomy, troublesome adventure called life'. (1952:202)

A virile, intense, and indefinable comradeship is established between the four men. At one moment they think that they have fallen into a ditch where they would be at the mercy of the first shell to hit them. Pradé already imagines his son's future irremediably compromised! In fact, they manage to get out: ' "So it wasn't on our ticket this time". . ."The war isn't over yet". . . Perhaps we shall be alive again tomorrow'. (1952:219)

The next day, the combatants find themselves outside a village evacuated by the men in the combat zone. Ducks, hens, eggs, the utensils of everyday life are still there, actualizing the permanent presence of those who have left and will soon return:

In front of us are some watering-cans with mushroom-shaped spouts, the kind I used to love as a boy; and it suddenly strikes me that man has emerged out of the depths of the past simply to invent a watering-can . . .

All we are worth, ourselves and the men opposite, is our mechanics, our courage and our cowardice; but the old race of men which we have chased away and which has only left behind its tools, its washing and its initials on the linen, seems to have risen, across the millennia, from the darkness we were in last night − slowly, greedily laden with all the scrap it has abandoned to us, the barrows and harrows, the biblical carts, the kennels and hutches, the empty ovens. (1952:222–4)

And the final image of the book is the sight of 'two old peasants', sitting on a bench. These are the peasants who, according to Molberg, constitute the formless mass, those who live from day to day, and yet here, in the face of the mechanical barbarity of war, they suddenly reveal their true meaning:

'Taking the sun, granpa?'. . .
    It is she who replies:
    'What else can we do? You, you're young; when you're old, there's nothing left but wear and tear . . .' (1952:224)

These are the same words that Malraux had put into the mouth of a soldier at the beginning of the book, 'I'm waiting for it to wear off', and, suddenly, the narrator understands in this eternal struggle between the risk of barbarity implied in culture and the fundamental life, age-old and patient, the true function of the latter. It is this fundamental life that makes possible and ensures each time the survival and rebirth of men:

Propped against the cosmos like a stone . . . Yet she smiles, a slow, pensive, delayed smile; beyond the football-pitch with its solitary goalposts, beyond the tank-turrets gleaming with dew like the bushes camouflaging them, she seems to be viewing death at a distance, with patience and even − oh, the mystery of those fluttering eyelids, the sharp shadows in the corner of her eyes! − even with irony.
    Open doors, washing, barns, man's imprint, biblical dawn in which the centuries jostle, how the whole dazzling mystery of the morning deepens into the mystery cropping out on those wasted lips of hers! Let the mystery of man only emerge from that enigmatic smile, and the resurrection of the earth becomes nothing more than a pulsating backcloth.
    I now know the meaning of the ancient myths about the living snatched from the dead. I can scarcely remember what fear is like; what I carry within me is the discovery of a simple, sacred secret.
    Thus, perhaps, did God look on the first man . . . (1952:224)

I shall stop my study here for several reasons that may not be independent of one another.
    The first is that *Les Noyers de l'Altenburg* is Malraux's last work to possess in any great degree the character of fiction. After that, as we know, Malraux was to undertake a new work, important no doubt but of an entirely different character: his studies on art. A deeper analysis would have to establish first of all the true nature of these studies, whether they were in effect scientific studies or rather essays in which the analysis of works of art provides Malraux with an *opportunity* to

pose, on the conceptual plane, a number of problems and to suggest a number of answers.

The second is that, in the following work at least, *Les Voix du Silence*, any idea of universal human value has entirely disappeared. (So too has any notion of the human condition as a potentiality for the revolutionary aspiration to dignity and the creation of history, or that of eternal man as an aspiration to happiness and resistance to barbarity – Kyo, May, Katow, Kassner, Manuel, as well as the prisoners and peasants of *Les Noyers de l'Altenburg*.)

The third reason is that with World War II there comes to an end not only the period on which our present research is based and of which this work marks the first stage, but also a particularly important period in the history of industrial, capitalist Europe: the period that I would like to call the great structural crisis of Europe, of which the two world wars, Italian fascism, the economic crisis of 1929–1933, and National Socialism were only the more important manifestations.

Since the end of World War II, in effect, a whole series of qualitative changes have occured in the economic, social, and cultural life of Western industrial societies, changes which, of course, we are unable to analyse here.

Let us mention, however, the two most important of these; the discovery of nuclear energy, with all the consequences that this involves on the level of military strategy and international politics, and, probably even more important, the creation of mechanisms of economic regulation and State intervention that have proved sufficiently effective to avoid, so far at least, any serious crisis of over-production – and it seems likely that they will avoid, perhaps for a long time, perhaps forever, the return of a crisis like that of 1929–1933. The history of Western capitalism, it seems to me, falls into three broad periods:

a) that of liberal capitalism and its rise in the second half of the nineteenth and first years of the twentieth century, a rise linked to the possibility of prolonged and continuous colonial expansion.

b) that of the great structural crisis in Western capitalism that extends from 1912 to about 1945, and which was caused in the first place by the gradual disappearance of possibilities of economic penetration in new countries (to which should be added, from 1917 onwards, the disappearance of two particularly important underdeveloped markets: the Russian market and later, on account of permanent civil wars, the Chinese market).

c) the emergence since World War II of an advanced capitalist society which, thanks to the creation of powerful mechanisms of State intervention and economic regulation, is able to dispense with the massive export of capital and invest in the home market.

We know the extent to which, beyond its particular importance for Malraux's work or for the history of his philosophical ideas, the end of World War II constitutes a turning-point of prime importance in the history of Western society as a whole. As I have already said, Malraux's ideological development is largely the expression of this change in the world in which he lived and wrote.

In this study, I have tried as far as possible to avoid value judgements of an aesthetic or political order, while being perfectly well aware, as I have already said elsewhere, that their total elimination is impossible and that the researcher may only try to reduce as far as possible the effects of these judgements on his work. I should like to say, however, that the close links that I have been able to establish between the development of Malraux's *oeuvre* and the cultural, social, and political history of Western Europe from the end of World War I, and the internal coherence of his works, which I have tried to bring out, seem to suggest that we are dealing with a particularly representative writer and that his development poses, in the double sense of its nature and of the dangers that it contains, the principal problems raised by the relations between culture and the most recent phase in the history of Western industrial societies.

The disappearance of revolutionary perspectives and hopes, the emergence of a world in which all important acts are confined to an élite of specialists (which we may call creators or technocrats according to whether we are dealing with the life of the mind or the economic, social, and political life), the reduction of the mass of men to mere objects of the action of this élite, without any real function in cultural creation or in social, economic, and political decision-making, the difficulty of pursuing imaginary creation in a world in which it cannot find support in universal human values — quite obviously, such problems concern not only the recent evolution of our society but also the last stage in Malraux's *oeuvre*. It should also be added, since at the beginning of this study I compared the theory of creative élites propounded by the later Malraux with the implicit position that emerges from Heidegger's *Sein und Zeit*, that there is, between the work of 1926 and those that followed World War II, between Heidegger's book and Malraux's aesthetic essays, a difference analogous with that which separates the capitalism of the 1920s, which was a capitalism in crisis, and the reorganized capitalism of today — the disappearance of the essential importance of *angst* (anxiety).

These are, however, merely hypotheses that require further analysis and later verification.

Is Malraux's *oeuvre* a more or less typical expression of the thought and feelings of a particular social group? Or does it belong to a wider structure comprising other *oeuvres* with which one might discover a structural relation? If so, what relation exists between these structures of the intellectual life, which we have still to discover, and the structures of the economic, social, political life between the two World Wars in France and in Western Europe? What are the relations between Malraux's development and that of other intellectuals and writers who also, at the same time, abandoned revolutionary values? What are the important *oeuvres* in French literature between the two Wars, written from a humanist point of view, that affirm the existence of universal human values? What are the structures of their worlds?

I have confined myself to enumerating these problems, to which I cannot for the moment bring a serious solution, in order to remind my readers that this study constitutes only a first, provisional and, above all, partial stage within the framework of a much wider research into French thought, literature, and society between the two Wars, a research that I will try to undertake in the years to come.

Note added 1965

This study had already been published when I realized that, in *L'Être et le néant* (1943:615–638), Sartre develops against Heidegger and against Malraux (to whom he attributes only the position of *L'Espoir* according to which 'death transforms life into destiny') an analysis very close to the one I developed in studying *Les Conquérants* and *La Voie royale*. No doubt, historical action enjoys no privilege in this radically individualistic work but, for Sartre, man defines himself by the fundamental project and the secondary projects that attach themselves to it, in the perspective of which the death to come is not a possibility of the subject but, on the contrary, an external given, an unforeseen, unexpected hindrance, which he must take into account, by preserving in it its specifically unexpected character. Thus these projects deprive the consciousness of death of any decisive importance until the day inevitable death destroys *retroactively* the value of these projects.

Excluding any conscious influence, the fact that two writers of this importance should develop in France, at so short a distance in time, positions so complex and so similar leads one to suspect the action of trans-individual and probably social action; but for the moment this observation simply poses a problem and I have no hypothesis that might help me to elucidate it.

NOTES and REFERENCES

1   This is also the order adopted by Malraux himself in the edition of his works published by Skira.

2   'How could I ever forget you, Princess of China?'. . .

      'Tell me,' he said, turning towards me, 'about the Princess of China.'

      I had never seen her?

      'Ah! Lassitude', murmured the prince, 'lassitude . . . Neither have I, poor soul . . .', and, after a moment of silence:

      'Let him be sent to the army.'

3   Here, as elsewhere in this study, the italics are mine.

4   Men came out, laden with magnificent objects on which one could make out silk and pearls: models, large richly dressed dolls, ancient toys . . . These soldiers belonged to the Afghan and Sartian troops, the most savage part of the army; they moved forward heavily, as if under a spell, murmuring to themselves. This murmuring became louder and louder until it became a great shout: 'The gods! The gods! THE GODS!' — You know that for several centuries the Masters of the Ports levied on all the marvels that lesser nations continually sent them a tithe of the rare objects intended for the Throne. Thick dust lay over certain of the underground chambers, the remains of the most beautiful flowers and rarest fruits of the previous century. Above, innumerable toys, piled one on top of another, stretched as far as the eye could see; the Princes of this dynasty had inherited a love of toys. For three centuries, the masters of the earth, bowing respectfully, had presented these puerile and complicated offerings to the King of Kings . . . In order to escape from the jostling crowd, each soldier held aloft the trophy he was carrying; and above the close-packed silhouettes, automata, mechanical animals and dolls moved slowly forward, black, reflecting from the light of the rising flames only the red glows caught by their false jewels.

      That night was without doubt one of the great nights of the world, one of those nights when the stunned gods abandon the earth to the wild geniuses of poetry. All night, do you hear, all night, in a long farandole, the hirsute soldiers walked round and round the incandescent palace and camp-fires, shouting, tenderly holding, like infants, these delicate toys, stroking as they went the automata, which lost their way in the pillaged gardens, and of which only the viols and flutes could be heard in the heat, as the shouts died down. . . Far from the flames, in the deepest shadows, the Chinese executioners and archers were secretly carrying away in their cupped hands the real pearls of the dead princes in order to sell them to the kingdoms of the South where the kings are painted. . .

5   'Now,' said Lust, 'to the empire of Death!'

      Pride protested.

      'Sir, I should be very much obliged if you would not make us look ridiculous. Everyone knows that "the Empire of Death" is called the Fantastic Kingdom.'

6   *Farfelu* is a favourite word of the author's, meaning whimsical, eccentric, dotty, bizarre, fey.

7   In view of the date (1920), the writers referred to are probably the Dadaists and early Surrealists led by Tristan Tzara.

8   The sins did not care for actions that could be performed by anybody; so they refused to use their feet and found it more appropriate to move by walking on their hands.

9   A schematization that nevertheless has a basis in reality. Indeed, it is difficult to imagine a writer creating an *oeuvre* possessing both the scope and structure of Malraux's novels after World War II (although even that is not inconceivable).

10   Indeed, it may be that Malraux encountered these, and other, problems through the existentialist and Marxist philosophies whose influence was becoming widespread in France; we shall have to undertake a study of these influences in the near future.

11   Where they do not express a purely hedonist aesthetic that reduces art to pleasure, eliminating any relation with transcendence.

12   André Malraux, *The Conquerors* (trans. Winifred Stephens Whale) 1956. Boston: Beacon Press. p. 1.

13   For some, to me incomprehensible, reason, the 'Suisse, Allemagne, Tchécoslovaquie, Autriche' of the original become, in the English translation, 'England, Belgium, the United States' (Tr.).

14   In the end, he leaves it to Chen-Dai to order Hong's execution and to Hong to assassinate Chen-Dai before his own arrest.

15   This passage is omitted from the English translation (Tr.).

16   Malraux has already told us that after the victory of the revolution, Garine might become a 'Mussolinian'. In the world of the novel, of course, this deprives his action of any authentic meaning. But the very existence of this threat, the danger of adopting the wrong course as a constituent element in the character — this is not the case in Borodin's character — derives from the fact that he does not seek values in themselves, but only as an indispensable element of meaningful action.

17   To avoid any misunderstanding, I should stress that death presents two *different* and *complementary* aspects for Malraux's heroes. According to circumstances, death has, in effect, an immanent, meaningful, or even transcendent and absurd reality in relation to action. As a reality immanent in action, death forms an essential element of action under the dual aspect of the risk of being killed that any serious historical action involves (in this respect, it is the same for all the revolutionaries — Klein, Borodin, Nicolaieff) and of the (for Garine, and later, for Perken) essential possibility of suicide that enables one to avoid decline in the case of defeat and reduction to passivity. (I shall return to the importance of suicide in Malraux's first two novels.)

But apart from this *immanent* and *meaningful* aspect, death is also, for the heroes as for all other men, a permanent threat, alien to any problem involving action and essentially unrelated to action. Like all men, Garine is threatened with death at any moment and even, which is the case in the novel, at the moment when his death is most absurd: the moment of victory.

And, of course, by its arrival, death will destroy retroactively the meaning that the individual had been able provisionally to find, as an individual, in historical action.

18 This is how he defines his action and his project − projects which he situates already in the past at the moment the narrative begins:

> 'Just to *be* a king means nothing; it's the building up of a kingdom that's worthwhile. I didn't act the fool with sabre-duels, and though, believe me, I'm a good shot, I hardly ever used my rifle. But I'm in close relations with almost all the chiefs of the unpacified tribes as far as Upper Laos. Fifteen years I've been at it, tackling them one after the other, brave men and sots. And now it's I whom they look up to, not the Siamese Government.'
>
> 'What do you want to make of them?'
>
> 'I wanted . . . First of all, a military force; a crude one, perhaps, but easy to bring up to scratch in a very short time. And when to await the struggle that's bound to come out here, either between the settlers and the natives, or between the Europeans themselves. Then I could set on foot the great adventure. You see, I want to survive for many men, and perhaps for a long time; to leave my mark upon the map of Asia. In the great game I'm playing against death I'd rather have twenty tribes to back me than a child . . . Yes, that is what I wanted just as my father coveted his neighbour's land − or I want women.' André Malraux, *The Royal Way* (trans. Stuart Gilbert) (1935) London: Methuen, pp. 83−84.

19 The difficulties of action and the fear of impotence also existed for Perken, Garine, and Grabot during the climactic periods of action as constituent elements of this action.

20 'Trotskyist' and 'Stalinist' are not to be regarded as absolutes. Trotsky never denied the value of discipline nor the Stalinists that of the revolutionary community. But each of these two tendencies, for political reasons that I have already outlined, stressed the priority of one of these values in relation to the other.

In *La Condition humaine*, Malraux does not take sides and is content to indicate the arguments in favour of each of these values and the consequences of their respective predominance, but it is obvious that his sympathies are with the Shanghai revolutionaries. In *L'Espoir*, on the other hand, even though in reality the problems existing in Spain were of similar kind to those that he had described in China, the conflict between discipline and the will to develop the revolution disappears entirely, the work being centred solely on the exclusive value of the first conceived as a military, not a political problem.

21 However, it is important, I think, to stress that by passing from the individual to the community, the problematic character of the

hero of the novel changes its nature to a certain extent; the individual problems of Kyo, May, and Katow are resolved in effect in *La Condition humaine* and their lives are entirely meaningful; it is the action of the group as a whole, on the other hand, that is problematic, on account of its attachment to the contradictory values of the immediate revolutionary action that creates the community and the discipline within the International, and the impossibility of conceptualizing the contradiction that results.

This leads, among other things, to an important change in the *dénouement: La Condition humaine* contains no 'conversion', no sudden awareness of the provisional, problematic character of the earlier search. The *dénouement* here is a maximum intensification of the situation that characterizes the whole narrative: an apotheosis of the individuals, the total failure of the group's external action, at least on the immediate plane (the future that is glimpsed in the final pages is not only, as I shall show, an added element, but it is the future of a different kind of community than that of the group of Shanghai revolutionaries).

It proved necessary in our discussion of this novel in Brussels to make one more thing clear.

Although, in the structure of *La Condition humaine*, the hero is constituted by the group of Shanghai revolutionaries, the world is constituted not only by Chiang Kai-shek, Ferral, and the explicitly, consciously counter-revolutionary forces, but also by the Communist leadership in Hankow which, although subjectively revolutionary, objectively favours, in the limited time that constitutes the action of the novel, the failure of the Shanghai revolutionaries and the victory of Chiang Kai-shek.

As for the link that binds the Shanghai group in the novel to the Hankow leadership – the fact they are both Communist groups opposed to capitalist oppression – it constitutes precisely that dialectical relation between the hero and the world that Lukács has so well described and which makes possible the novel structure.

22 In the last resort, when faced with the resistance of the Shanghai militants, the Party agrees that the arms that have not already been handed in should only be buried.

23 It should be stressed, however, that on the conceptual plane, Malraux does not follow the position of Trotsky and the opposition, who spoke of the 'treason' of the bureaucracy, since he sees in the attitude of the International – as, indeed, the International explicitly stated – a provisional *tactic* about whose correct or incorrect character it left discussion open. Moreover, the last part of the novel defends the 'official' view of 'socialism in one country' and indicates that the construction of the USSR and the ultimate struggle of the Communist Party integrate and continue the struggle of the Shanghai militants.

24 Borodin himself appears in *La Condition humaine*, but he is not at all the same character as in *Les Conquérants*. He is now the leader of the Communist International, the bureaucrat as seen by

Trotsky, and has nothing but the name in common with the militant so closely bound up with the revolution in *Les Conquérants*, the homologue of this character being represented in *La Condition humaine*, as I have just said, by the Shanghai militants.

25   We must remember that in *Les Conquérants* Chen Dai also spoke of the *sons* of his friends whom he had urged to enter the Cadet School.

26   André Malraux, *Man's Estate* (trans. Alastair Macdonald) (1968) London: Hamish Hamilton, p. 7.

27   Indeed, he says as much in a conversation he later has with old Gisors, his spiritual father:

'I'm unbelievably lonely,' he said, looking hard at Gisors.

Gisors was perturbed . . . What he failed to understand was why Chen, who had presumably seen some of the terrorists since the crime, as he had just been seeing Kyo again, should seem so out of touch with them.

'What about the others?' he said . . .'

'They don't know.'

'That it's you who did it?'

'Yes, they know that: that's not the thing.'

He was silent again. Gisors refrained from questioning him. At last Chen went on:

'. . . that it's the first time.'. . .

'You haven't ever killed anybody, have you?' (1968a:45–6)

This conversation brings out yet another kinship with Garine. The first woman he slept with was a prostitute (elsewhere in the book, May says that Chen 'loathed love'). The nature of his relation with the prostitutes he slept with is a synthesis of domination and solidarity:

'What were your feelings afterwards?' asked Gisors.

Chen clenched his fingers.

'Pride.'

'At being a man?'

'At not being a woman.'

There was no bitterness in his voice now, but a curious contempt.

'I think what you mean is,' he continued, 'that I must have felt . . . cut off?'. . .

'Yes. Terribly. And you are right to bring women into it. One may feel great contempt for the man one kills. But less for other people.'

'For those who do not kill?'

'For those who do not kill: the uninitiated!' (1968a:47)

Similarly, much more than a Chinese, he is above all like Garine an intellecutal, a man whose life is structured by an idea:

'I am Chinese,' Chen answered bitterly.

'No,' thought Gisors. Except, possibly as far as sex was concerned, Chen was not Chinese. The migrants of all nationalities, who thronged Shanghai, had shown Gisors how national man remains even in the nature of his attempts to shake off his nationality; but Chen no longer belonged to China, even in the manner of his renunciation: complete liberty of thought had given him complete freedom. (1968a:47)

28   In view of the special importance of the love between Kyo and May in Malraux's *oeuvre*, and the difficulty of conveying it through a conceptual analysis, I will let the text speak for itself by quoting it at length.

29   This is also Saint-Exupéry's view. In the present state of the world, the conquerors open the way to the technocrats and are eliminated and replaced by them.

30   This is a frequent phenomenon is the history of literature. It is the result of the interference in imaginary creation, which tends to follow its own laws and orientates itself towards its own coherence, of the writer's ideological convictions; the sociological historian of literature might quote similar cases from the works of the greatest writers (for example, Goethe or Balzac).

31   In order to avoid any misunderstanding, I should perhaps make it clear that I am using the term problematic character not in the sense of one that 'poses problems', but in the sense of a character whose existence and values confront him with insoluble problems, of which he cannot be clearly and rigorously conscious (it is this that distinguishes the novel hero from the tragic hero).

32   The epic moving towards an inevitable affirmation of reconciliation between the individual and the community and the lyrical, which is present as a complementary aspect of the postulated and non-organic character of this reconciliation.

33   André Malraux, *Days of Contempt* (trans. Haakon M. Chevalier) (1936) London: Victor Gollancz, p. 53.

34   Just as Saint-Exupéry had probably developed his image of the conqueror in implicit reference to Malraux's.

35   The continuation of their struggle in the Communist International and in the building up of the Soviet Union strikes me, as I have already said, as being somewhat artificial in terms of the novel.

36   We have only to think of the significance of the militants' children we encounter in the novel: Hemmelrich's child prevents him from taking part in the struggle and is killed during the repression; while Pei, who acts as a kind of child for Chen, joins the Communists in building up the USSR, thus separating himself from the man who had hoped to see his work continued by him.

37   André Malraux, *Days of Hope* (trans. Alastair Macdonald) (1968) London: Hamish Hamilton, p. 433.

38   It is interesting to note that, at about the same time, Sartre approached this same problem from a diametrically opposite point of view in his story, *L'Enfance d'un Chef*. In spite of the opposition between these two texts it is important to observe that the problem was of concern to a number of intellectuals.

39   André Malraux, *The Walnut Trees of Altenburg* (trans. A. W. Fielding) (1952) London: John Lehmann, p. 20.

40 The narrator is Alsatian, which explains the fact that in 1914 his
    father was a German officer.
41 Though the seizure of power in 1917 was carried out under the
    direction of Lenin — the transposition does simplify things to
    some extent.
42 The narrator's uncle and organizer of the Altenburg discussions.

3 The *Nouveau Roman* and Reality

After the last two papers by writers,[1] I would now like to speak to you from a very different point of view, that of the sociologist. There is, in effect, between the point of view of the sociologist and that of the writer a difference similar to that existing between the point of view of the runner or the athlete and that of the psychologist or physiologist who studies the psychical or physiological structure of their behaviour.

Nevertheless, the two approaches may be complementary as well as contradictory. Not to mention the ever-present possibility that a sociologist or a critic or, respectively, a psychologist or a physiologist, might be mistaken and develop erroneous theories, it may well be that the runner or athlete does not know the psychical and physiological structures that enable him to achieve his performances, or that the writer is not entirely conscious of the mechanism of his creation — which is quite independent of the respective quality of these performances or his creation. Fortunately, it happens very often that the two perspectives complement and illuminate one another. This will to a large degree be the case today, for although Nathalie Sarraute and Alain Robbe-Grillet are neither sociologists nor critics, they speak to us as theoreticians — which means that they are doing, brilliantly and with much insight, the work of literary critics.

Speaking third and as a sociologist, what I have to say will therefore, to a large degree, be merely a complement to the two papers you have just heard. It would be good, nevertheless, to begin by stressing what, in these papers, seems to me, not only valid, but particularly important, and also what separates me — though, in the last resort, only on secondary points — from Nathalie Sarraute's analysis.

Let us begin with a point that is common to the two papers: their profession of faith in literary realism. In effect, while many critics and a large section of the public see in the *nouveau roman* a set of purely formal experiments and, generally speaking, an attempt to evade social reality, two of the principal representatives of this school have just told you, on the contrary, that their work was born out of an effort, as rigorous and as radical as possible, to grasp, in its most essential way, the reality of our time. My commentary on the papers and the work of the two writers is offered primarily by way of illustrating and concretizing this affirmation, which seems to me both important and valid.

Another element common to the two papers that it seems to me useful to stress is the declaration that if these two writers have adopted a different form from that of the nineteenth-century novelists it is primarily because they had to describe and express a different human reality (the sociologist would say social reality, in so far as for him all human reality is social).

Lastly, Nathalie Sarraute's paper seems to me to reveal remarkable penetration and truth when she shows how psychical habits, old mental structures and categories that persist in the consciousness of most people, prevent them from grasping a new reality, which is essential in so far as it structures in effect men's everyday lives, even if many of them are not aware of the fact. The point on which I fear her practice as a writer has prevented her from grasping the importance of social and historical reality is the way in which Nathalie Sarraute sees the process of change in reality that has made necessary the passage from the classical novel to the 'new novel', and the forces that have helped to bring this about. I fear that, in this process, Nathalie Sarraute overestimates the importance of writers and implicitly underestimates that of all other men. Speaking (quite rightly) of the progress made in literary research, Nathalie Sarraute seems to see such research rather too much, in my opinion, in terms of the history of physics and chemistry. It would appear that for her there exists a human reality given once and for all (analagous to cosmic reality) which writers, like scientists, explore one after the other, thus creating from one generation to the next a mere shift of interest towards new sectors, which then have to be explored as the old problems are solved. It is because Balzac and Stendhal analysed the psychology of the character and, by that very fact, generalized and depreciated it, that, according to Nathalie Sarraute, such psychology no longer has any interest and that later writers – Joyce, Proust, Kafka – had to turn to finer, more subtle realities, thus opening a way that the novelists of today must in turn strive to achieve.

In fact, it seems to me that on this point Robbe-Grillet has seen things more clearly. There is, in the human domain, no immutable reality, given once and for all, that is simply there to be explored with increasing subtlety from one generation of writers and artists to another. The essence of human reality is itself dynamic and changes through history; moreover, this change is, to an unequal degree, of course, the work of *all* men and, although writers play their part, it is neither an exclusive nor a preponderant one.

Although the history and psychology of the character are becoming more and more difficult to describe without falling into mere anecdote, this is not only because Balzac, Stendhal, or Flaubert have already described it, but because we are living in a different society from the one in which they lived, a society in which the individual as such and, implicitly, his biography and psychology have lost all their truly primordial importance and have fallen to the level of mere anecdote. As Robbe-Grillet said in his paper, if the *nouveau roman* describes relations between a jealous man and his wife, the wife's lover and the objects around them in a different way, it is not because the author is looking for an original form at all cost, but because the very structure in which all these elements participate has changed its nature. In effect, the wife and one should add the lover and the jealous man himself have become objects and, within the totality of this structure and all the essential structures of contemporary society, human feelings (which are and always have been the expression of internal human relations and relations between men and the material world, natural or manufactured) now express relations in which objects have a permanence and autonomy that characters are gradually losing.

After these preliminary remarks on two papers that seem to me to be particularly important for an understanding of contemporary literature, allow me – since I am also speaking to you as a sociologist – to raise the problem of the nature of the social transformations that have in fact created the need for a new novel form, and also to illustrate with a few examples the way in which certain essential features of this new human reality are expressed in the work of Nathalie Sarraute and Robbe-Grillet.

It is not possible, of course, within such a brief space, to provide an over-all history of Western societies from the beginning of the nineteenth century. I will have to content myself therefore with mentioning a few points of particular importance for the problem confronting us today, that of the *nouveau roman.*

I shall take as my starting-point a correlation that seems to me, at first sight, to be especially fruitful.

On the literary plane, the essential transformation concerns primarily – Nathalie Sarraute and Robbe-Grillet have just said as much – the character/objects structural unity, modified in the direction of *a more or less radical disappearance of the character and a corresponding strengthening of the autonomy of objects.*

Now, our research into novel form in the literary sociology group in Brussels University has already led us to the hypothesis that the novel form is, of all literary forms, the most immediately and most directly linked to the economic structure in the narrow sense of the term, to the structures of exchange and market production. From this viewpoint, it is significant that, from 1867 and even from 1859, whereas no one was yet thinking of the literary problems raised by Nathalie Sarraute and Robbe-Grillet, Karl Marx, studying the principal transformations introduced into the structure of social life by the appearance and development of the economy, situated them precisely on the level of the inert individual-object relationship and emphasized the gradual transferance of the coefficient of reality, autonomy, and activity from the first to the second. This is the famous Marxist theory of the *fetishization of commodities* or, to use the term adopted almost unanimously in Marxist literature since Lukács, *reification*.

However, encouraging and significant as the similarities between Marx's theoretical analyses in the nineteenth century and the discoveries of a number of contemporary writers may be for our hypothesis, they nevertheless seem to me to be still too generalized to satisfy sociological research. Indeed, we still have to ask ourselves why a gap of almost a century separates the elucidation of the phenomenon of reification and its appearance in the novel without character.

Basically, the question that presents itself is the following: does there exist an intelligible relation or a homology between the history of reificational structures and the history of fictional structures? In order to answer this question, we must take into account, it seems to me, four decisive elements whose nature can briefly be described as follows:

a) reification as a permanent psychological process working for several centuries uninterruptedly in Western market societies. To this can be added three particular elements that determine the concrete aspect of reificational structures in the history of these socieites, and, by that fact, the periodization of these societies.

b) the liberal economy which, up to the beginning of the twentieth century, still maintains the essential function of the individual in the economic life and, therefore, in social life as a whole.

c) the development, at the end of the nineteenth century and above all at the beginning of the twentieth, of trust, monopolies, and finance capital, which introduces a qualitative change in the nature of Western capitalism, a change which Marxist theoreticians have described as the passage from liberal capitalism to imperialism. The consequence of this passage — the qualitative turning-point of which is situated at about the end of the first decade of the twentieth century — was primarily, from the point of view that concerns us here, *the suppression of all essential importance attributed to the individual and the individual life within the economic structures and, therefore, in social life as a whole.*

d) the development, during the years preceding World War II and above all since the end of the war, of state intervention in the economy, and the creation, through this intervention, of self-regulatory mechanisms that make contemporary society *a third qualitative stage* in the history of Western capitalism.

I take it that the concepts of liberal economy, monopolies, trusts, finance capital, and state intervention are more or less known, so I shall be content here to say something about reification.

What do we mean by this word? As Marx describes it in the first chapter of *Capital* in the term *fetishism of commodities*, the phenomenon is extremely simple and easy to understand.

Capitalist society in which all goods are produced for the market differs essentially from all earlier (and probably later) forms of social organization of production. These differences assume of course many different aspects. However, these are usually derived from a primary fundamental difference: the absence, in liberal capitalist society, of any organism capable of regulating in a concious way both production and distribution within a given social unit.

Such organisms existed in every form of precapitalist society, whether a primitive society living from hunting and fishing, or, as in the Middle Ages, the peasant family or even the unit constituted by the Lord's castle and a number of peasant families in the village, forced to supply either labour rent (*corvées*) or ground rent; or even, up to a point, the market economy of the European city in its beginnings (though here the plan existed in the form of a sort of unthematized and translucid consciousness and a study in depth might well find the first manifestations of the phenomenon of reification in such a society).

This regulation of production might be traditional, religious, oppressive, etc. It nevertheless had a conscious character (or at least a translucent one as in the case of the medieval city). Similarly, it is conscious in a socialist or socialist-type society in which production is organized by a central planning commission.

In classical liberal society, on the other hand, there is no conscious regulation of production and consumption at any level. In such a society, of course, production is nevertheless regulated and, in the long term, one produces only the quantity of corn, shoes, or cannons corresponding to demand and the supply of money, and, consequently, to the actual consumption of the society. But this regulation operates in an *implicit* way, outside the consciousness of individuals, imposing itself on them as the mechanical action of an outside force. The law of supply and demand operates through the market, and above all through the crises that periodically correct imbalances.

On the immediate level of individual consciousnesses, the economic life assumes the aspect of the rational egotism *homo economicus*, of the exclusive search for maximum profit with no consideration for the problems of human relations with others and above all with no consideration for society as a whole. From this viewpoint, other men become for the seller or buyer objects like any other objects, mere means that enable him to achieve his ends, whose only important human quality will be their capacity to make contacts and produce constricting obligations.

However, since the regulations imposed by society as a whole operate nevertheless, their existence must be expressed in some way and when eliminated from men's consciousnesses these regulations reappear in society as new properties of inert objects, which are added to their natural properties: their exchange value and price.

Of course, trees are and have always been green in the summer and leafless in winter, large or small, hardy or worm-eaten, etc. In a market economy, however, they have, in addition to all that, a property that they had in no natural economy (and which, in spite of appearances to the contrary, they do not have in a planned economy): that of being *worth* a particular sum of money, of having a *price* linked to supply and demand that determines in the last resort the number of trees that will be cut down and used for production in a given year — and the same goes, of course, for all other commodities.

Thus the whole set of fundamental values in the psychical life, values that, in precapitalist social forms were — and, in future forms, will be, we hope — constituted by trans-individual feelings (morality, aesthetics, charity, and faith) disappears from individual consciousnesses in the economic sector, whose weight and importance are constantly increasing in the social life, and delegates its functions to a new property of inert objects — their price.

The consequences of this change are considerable, but I cannot analyse them here.[2] They also involve, however, positive aspects; they make possible the development of a certain number of fundamental ideas in Western European culture (ideas of equality, tolerance, and individual liberty, among others). But they have gradually increased the passivity of individual consciousnesses and the elimination of the qualitative element in relations between men, on the one hand, and between men and nature, on the other.

This phenomenon involves the abolition, the reduction to the implicit, of an extremely important sector of individual consciousnesses. For this sector is substituted a new property, of purely social origin, belonging to inert objects, in the sense that such objects penetrate the market in order to be exchanged. Thus the active functions of men are transferred to objects. It is this phantasmagorical illusion (which Marx compares with the point of view of the Shakespearean character for whom to be able to read and write was a natural quality and beauty the result of merit) that has been designated by the extremely fruitful terms of *fetishism of commodities* and, later, of *reification*.

In the structure of the liberal society analysed by Marx, reification thus reduced to the implicit all trans-individual values, transforming them into properties of things and left as essential, manifest human reality only the individual, deprived of all immediate, concrete, and conscious links with the whole.

A balanced world corresponding to this structure would, if pushed to its limit, be that of *Robinson Crusoe*, the isolated individual confronted by a world of objects, plants, and animals (and in which other men exist only as wage-earners, as represented by the character of Friday). However, as Lukács observed in a much more developed analysis, man cannot remain human and also accept the absence of concrete, univocal contacts with other men. Thus the humanist creation that really corresponded to the reificational structure of liberal society was the history of the problematic individual as expressed in Western literature from *Don Quixote* to Stendhal and Flaubert, by way of Goethe (and, as Girard has shown, with certain modifications, to Proust and, in Russia, to Dostoievsky).

As Robbe-Grillet has just said, the classical novel is the novel in which objects have a primordial importance but in which they exist only through their relations with *individuals*. The two later periods of Western capitalist society, the imperialist period – which is situated approximately between 1912 and 1945 – and the present period of capitalist organization can be defined on the structural plane by the gradual disappearance of the individual as an essential reality and, correlatively, by the increasing independence of objects, in the case of the first, and, in the case of the second, by the constitution of this world of objects – in which the human being has lost all essential reality either as an individual or as a community – as an autonomous world with its own structuration which alone enables the human being to express himself, occasionally and with difficulty.

I should now like to formulate a hypothesis which, of course, will have to be checked against later research. It seems to me that to the last two periods in the history of the economy and of reification in Western societies correspond two great periods in the history of the novel form: the first is characterized by the dissolution of the character and contains some extremely important *oeuvres*, such as those of Joyce,

Kafka, Musil, Sartre's *La Nausée,* Camus's *L'Étranger*, and, very probably, as one of its most radical manifestations, the work of Nathalie Sarraute; the second, which is only beginning to find its literary expression and of which Robbe-Grillet is one of the most authentic and most brilliant representatives, is precisely marked by the appearance of an autonomous world of objects, with its own structure and its own laws and through which alone human reality can still to a certain extent express itself.

Approaching now the concrete *oeuvre* of the two novelists, I would like to begin by observing that writing at the same period, our own, what they say about reality is not perhaps – despite everything that separates them – so very different.

The opposition between Nathalie Sarraute and Robbe-Grillet lies rather in what interests them, in what they are looking for, than in what they observe. Nathalie Sarraute is still – in the most advanced, most extreme form – a novelist of the period that I have characterized as being that of the dissolution of the character. The over-all structures of the social world do not interest her very much; she seeks everywhere the authentic human being, the immediate experience, whereas Robbe-Grillet seeks the human being as an exteriorized expression, as a reality inserted in an over-all structure.

But once one has formulated this difference, their observations seem to me to be very close. In seeking immediate experience, Nathalie Sarraute observes that this experience no longer exists in exteriorizations, which are all, almost without exception, inauthentic, distorted, and deformed. So, confronted by this extreme dissolution of the character, she limits the world of her works to the only domain in which she can still find the reality that seems to her to be essential (although, of course, here too she finds it deformed and exacerbated by the impossibility of exteriorization), to the feelings and human experience *anterior* to all expression, to what she calls tropisms, sub-conversation, sub-creation. In this sense, she seems to me (and I hope she will not mind my saying so) to be a writer who expresses an essential aspect of contemporary reality in a form for which she no doubt creates a new modality, but which is still that of the writers of the disappearance of the character – Kafka, Musil, Joyce, whom indeed she often hails as predecessors.

Nathalie Sarraute is interested above all in psychology and interhuman relations; she is not a victim of the reifying illusion and is still aware of the fact that all aspects, even the most false and inauthentic interhuman relations, those that do most to prevent communication, are the result, in the end, of a degradation of the human, of the psychical. I would have liked to have been able to add that she is aware that the increasing autonomy of objects is merely the external manifestation of this degradation; but this would be untrue, for she shows very little interest in any kind of exteriorization and does not record the new status of objects in social life. I need only take as one example among many the forty pages devoted to a door-handle at the beginning of *Le Planetarium*. At no point does the author accord the least autonomy to this handle; everything is immediately translated into the psychical reactions of the old woman, the nephew, her father, her mother, and their friends. The *essential* structure of the object/individual relation still remains the same as in the classical novel. Nathalie Sarraute has merely recorded the psychical transformations that constitute the content of this relation; from this point of view, there is no essential difference between the 'function within the work' of the door handle and that of all the *external* manifestations of men, such as, for example, that of the famous writer who wrote 'an essay on Husserl' or that of Germaine Lemaire in the bookshop episode.

Conversely, Robbe-Grillet, who concentrates on the external manifestations of the social life, does not register the essentially human and psychical character of the relations that lie at the origin of reification and of the increasing autonomy of objects. One might characterize the writings of these two authors by transposing to the *nouveau roman* the Lukácsian distinction between the novel of abstract idealism centred on the external action of the hero and his inadequacy in the world, and the psychological novel of disillusion centred on the impossibility of action, caused by an inadequacy of a complementary type. However, it should be stressed that in either case these two types of the same structure undergo a modification due to the disappearance of the character.[3]

Robbe-Grillet expresses this same reality of contemporary society in an essentially new form.

For him, too, the disappearance of the character is an acquired fact, but he observes that this character has already been replaced by another autonomous reality (which does not interest Nathalie Sarraute): the reified world of objects. And as he too is seeking human reality — this is another point common to the two writers — he observes that this reality, which can no longer be found in the over-all structures as spontaneous, immediately experienced, reality can be rediscovered only in so far as it is still expressed in the structure and properties of objects.

You will understand why, as a sociologist, I think that in our period, with the limits that the contraction of the human world imposes on all cultural creation, the works of Nathalie Sarraute and Robbe-

Grillet are particularly important phenomena. I do think, however, that the work of Robbe-Grillet (I hope too that he will not mind my saying so) is so perhaps not so much by what he intended to do as by what he has in fact done.

For it may be that within the framework I have indicated, that of the autonomous essentially real and humanly alien world of things, Robbe-Grillet is still seeking psychological realities: the Oedipus complex in *Les Gommes*, an obsession in *Le Voyeur*, a feeling of jealousy in the novel of that name and, perhaps, a psychoanalytical treatment in *L'Année dernière à Marienbad*. But the important thing seems to me that these intentions – supposing them to have been effective – have managed to become incorporated in the work only to the extent that they could become linked to an otherwise essential analysis of the over-all structures of social reality.

The Oedipus complex remains an external ornament in *Les Gommes;* Mathias's obsession, the husband's jealousy are merely starting-points, raw material enabling the writer to express otherwise essential structures, which might have been expressed equally well on the basis of different feelings; the relations between the man and the woman in *L'Année dernière à Marienbad* become the expression of human relations as a whole. Furthermore, at the risk of disappointing most critics who have concentrated on the formal problems of his works, I will say that on reading Robbe-Grillet's writings I have had the impression that formal problems, while extremely important, have never possessed an autonomous character. Robbe-Grillet has something to say and, like all true writers, naturally seeks the forms best suited to expressing it. The content of his writing cannot be separated from their literary creation nor their literary creation from his work as a whole. Much has been said about the formal problems of Robbe-Grillet's novels. Perhaps it is time to speak of their content.

It is not, of course, a question of finding in these novels an esoteric content. Robbe-Grillet's formal research is an attempt to make the content as manifest, as accessible as possible, and if critics and readers have so much difficulty in grasping it, it is not the fault of the writer but that of the mental habits, preconceived feelings, and pre-established judgements with which most of them approach the act of reading.

Robbe-Grillet began to publish his work in 1953, with a sort of detective novel called *Les Gommes.* In this work he still preserves to a very large degree the traditional schema of the genre (an attempted murder, which in this case fails, a police investigation, etc.), within which he introduces a new content. Naturally enough, this involves a number of fairly important formal modifications. Nevertheless, it seems to me that it is this disparity between the new content and the still only partially renewed form that leads Robbe-Grillet to recall in a whole series of peripheral details what he wanted to say. I am referring to the allusions to the Oedipus myth that proliferate in a way more or less external to the main body of the work (the motifs of the curtains, the decoration of a chimney, the enigma of the sphinx, the passage concerning the possible existence of a son of the murdered man, etc.), in order to draw the readers attention to the fact that he is dealing not with a mere detective novel of the usual kind, but a book whose essential content is related to that of Greek tragedy. Of course, these allusions would have been useless (and nothing similar is to be found in Robbe-Grillet's later works) if the form of the work had been sufficiently adequate to convey the content. In what, indeed, does the kinship that Robbe-Grillet wishes to establish between *Les Gommes* and the Oedipus myth consist? It seems to me, in the last resort, to be somewhat slender and even debatable; the book certainly does not take up the myth itself. It is almost certain that Daniel Dupont was not murdered by his own son; at any rate, there is nothing in the book to make such a hypothesis plausible. The kinship resides in the fact that, in each case, there is a concatenation of events unfolding in accordance with an ineluctable necessity, quite unaffected by men's intentions and acts. Structurally, however, the necessity of ancient tragedy, which results from the conflict between the wills of the gods and men's efforts, and transforms human life into destiny, has very little in common (and Robbe-Grillet, who later abandons any allusion to this tragedy, probably realized as much himself) with the mechanical and inevitable process that unfolds within a world in which individuals in search of liberty have lost all reality and importance.

The content of the work is precisely this mechanical and ineluctable necessity that governs both relations between men and relations between men and things in a world that resembles a modern machine deprived of self-regulatory mechanisms. A clandestine, anti-government organization, having decided one day to kill a man, seizes one Daniel Dupont. Unfortunately, and this can happen in the most perfected of mechanisms, there is a miscalculation: Daniel Dupont switched on his office light too soon; the surprised assassin aimed badly and caused only a slight wound to the arm. Dupont, who knows he is a marked man, and who has influential connections in the government, allows people to believe, in order to protect himself, that the assassination has succeeded, and goes into hiding for a time, thus hoping to escape the vigilance of his assassins. A detective is sent to investigate a crime which, in reality, did not take place. It would seem that the fatal, mechanical character of the process has been disturbed, that a deviation from the norm has occurred. In reality, this is an illusion: the process is fatal and the mechanism perfect. For by the simple play of events, without anyone being aware of it or wishing it, the detective kills the so-called victim who thus becomes a real victim; an investigation of a real assassination can now take place. Meanwhile, the group of assassins continues its work even being aware of their mistake, and next day kills another man, Albert Dupont.

At this point, a last question might be asked. Why the title, *Les Gommes* (*The Erasers*), whose only connection with the action seems to be that, on several occasions, Wallace the detective goes into a stationer's to buy one. It seems to me that, as with the allusions to the Oedipus myth, we are dealing here with a reminder that is fairly external to the content of the novel: on an immediate level, the self-regulations that erase the 'failure', on a more general level the mechanism of a society that erases any trace of living disorder and reality from the individual. These same themes, but on an incomparably higher literary level, are to be found again in the author's second novel, and the one that aroused the liveliest discussions among literary critics: *Le Voyeur.* Some of you will remember the first, vehement, and indignant article by E. Henriot in *Le Monde*, and of his later *volte-face* when he proposed to place the book among the ten best works to take on one's holiday.

Le Voyeur poses the same problems as *Les Gommes*, but on a much more radical level and in a way that involves profound formal transformations. Naturally, it is these transformations alone that have attracted the attention of critics, who at the level of content have seen little more than an anecdote, the account of a mere incident that is of no interest to them or which, at most, leaves them shocked; and naturally, if one does not set out from the content that justifies and necessitates them, the 'formal' modifications might well seem arbitrary or artificial. Few critics, to my knowledge, have so much as raised the simple question of the title, *Le Voyeur*, which nevertheless indicates clearly enough the content of the book, and considered it on the level it deserves. For who is the voyeur? Quite obviously, the term applies only in a quite partial way to Mathias, the commercial traveller, who has in fact committed the murder around which the book is centred. One critic remarked that the term applied much more to young Marek. But there is a weighty objection to this interpretation: it would be difficult, in effect, to make young Marek the book's principal character.

We have only to ask what the content of the book is, however, to see that the answer becomes immediately clear. Of course, it is not simply the account of an incident, the murder of a little girl. There would be nothing new in this in relation to the traditional novel.

On the most immediate level, the author retranscribes the account that the commercial traveller Mathias tries to reconstitute from his twenty-four-day stay on an island where he had gone to sell watches. Mathias, who during this stay killed a little girl, is obsessed by the memory of this murder and the fear of being arrested. So his account is characterized at the outset by the two elements: on the one hand, a wish to give a plausible, fully accounted for version of his stay on the island by eliminating any reference to the murder, and, on the other hand, the fear of being discovered and arrested, which is expressed in his obsession with handcuffs and anything that reminds him of the 'flat figure eight' whose form they have for him.

This fear deforms the intentional structure of the narrative, preventing it from following a trajectory in accordance with the original intention, and constantly brings it back, either to the murder of the little girl or to certain events that occurred in Mathias's childhood and which, in his personal experience (Robbe-Grillet makes use here, to some extent, of psychoanalysis), are linked to the murder, thus giving it its psychological signification.

This content explains the style of the work and in particular the constant fluctuation within a single sentence between different characters and events that occurred at different times.

On an immediate level, therefore, the voyeur is *Mathias himself*, since the narrative takes place, not at the time he commits the crime, but later, when he is trying to construct a version of his day on the island that will eliminate any memory of the crime, although his vision is continually brought back, either to the crime itself, or to the various events and objects associated with it.

However, Mathias's great discovery, a discovery that he generally makes in the course of the narrative,[4] is that, not only is it impossible for him to conceal a murder to which his obsessional fear constantly brings him back, but that all effort is pointless since he is using an entirely false representation of social reality. In effect, Mathias begins by discovering that on the island there are two persons who were witnesses to the murder (this is certainly true in the case of one of these two people and highly probable in the case of the other), and who both persist in demonstrating the incorrectness of his statements whenever they are tending to conceal his act. This observation arouses a certain anxiety in him, of a temporary kind however, for he realizes soon enough that although both witnesses may be anxious to correct his statements, they do so only out of concern for the truth and have no

intention of denouncing him: *they are simply voyeurs*. Soon, Mathias
discovers that all the inhabitants of the island who, in this novel as in
any work of art, constitute, not a partial sector of a total world, but
that world itself, might very easily, with very little effort, discover the
murder, but that they are no more interested in doing so than young
Marek or little Maria. Basically, this murder, like the one in *Les
Gommes*, has become part of the order of things and, in so far as the
murdered girl was not like the other inhabitants of the island and
represented an element of spontaneity and disorder, her disappearance
even comes as a source of relief to them.[5]

Thus the world is made up solely of passive voyeurs who neither
wish nor can intervene in the life of society in order to transform it
qualitatively or to make it more human. The only man who was able to
think for a moment that the murder of the child was a punishable act
and one that might eliminate him from social life was Mathias himself
who, at the end of the novel, realizing his error, rejects the possibilities
of escape offered to him and waits quietly until the following morning
before catching the boat that will take him back to the mainland.

In this way, murder is made part of the universal order, categorized
in *Les Gommes* by the self-regulation that eliminates any possibility of
change arising from an unpredictable element in the individual
temperament, from an unexpected individual fault, and, in *Le Voyeur,*
by the passivity of all members of society.[6]

Perhaps I should make a few remarks here (unnecessary as they may
be) in order to avoid any possible misunderstanding. The theme of
these two novels, the disappearance of any importance and any
meaning from individual action, makes them in my opinion two of the
most realistic works of contemporary fiction. There might, however, be
readers or critics who would oppose me with an argument apparently
dictated by common sense: it is not true that whenever a murderer fails
to kill his victim a social mechanism corrects his mistake, just as it is
not true that when a commercial traveller murders a little girl, the
neighbours take no notice and the authorities do nothing to arrest him
and bring him to justice.

In an immediate way, these objections are well founded of course;
the problem, however, is posed on a much more radical level. There are
innumerable everyday crimes against the human being that are part of the
social order itself, which are accepted or tolerated by the law of society
and by the psychical structure of its members. Formerly, in earlier social
forms, the existence of these inhuman elements (one has only to think
of feudal privileges or sealed letters) could and did, at a certain stage of
social evolution, cause such indignation among members of certain

social groups and among the writers and thinkers who acted as their spokesmen (one has only to think of Voltaire or Lessing, for example), that it brought about a social transformation that attempted to make the survival of such practices impossible. These may in time cause other injustices and other inhuman practices, but these too will arouse indignation, and so on.

What Robbe-Grillet is indicating, what constitutes the subject of his first two novels, is the great social and human transformation brought about by the appearance of two new, extremely important phenomena — on the one hand, *the self-regulations* of society and, on the other hand, the *increasing passivity*, the character of 'voyeurs', that individuals are gradually assuming in modern society, the absence of any *active* participation in social life, what, in its most visible manifestation, modern sociologists call depoliticization, but which is really a much more fundamental phenomenon that might be designated, according to a progressive gradation, by such terms as: depoliticization, desacralization, dehumanization, reification.

It is this same reification which, on an even more radical level, is the object of Robbe-Grillet's third novel, *La Jalousie*. The very term used by Lukács indicated that the disappearance of all importance and all meaning from the actions of individuals[7], their transformation into voyeurs, into purely passive observers, were merely the superficial manifestations of a fundamental phenomenon, that of reification, of the transformation of human beings into things to the extent that it becomes increasingly difficult to distinguish them from things. It is on this level that Robbe-Grillet takes up the analysis of contemporary society in *La Jalousie*. This novel is written from the point of view of a jealous spectator, probably the husband, who is looking through a venetian blind (in French, *une jalousie*), the very title of the novel indicating that it is impossible in this world to separate the feeling from the object. The whole work shows the increasing autonomy of objects that are the sole concrete reality and outside which human realities and feelings can have no autonomous existence. The presence of the jealous man is indicated only by that of a third chair, a third glass, etc.

Several passages in the novel express the impossibility of separating the psychical, knowledge, feeling from the object:

> It takes a glance at her empty though stained plate to discover that she has not neglected to serve herself . . . Now the boy clears away the plates. It then becomes impossible to check again the stains in A. . .'s plate — or their absence, if she has not served herself.[8]

But what is more important than such details is the structure in which objects have acquired their own, autonomous reality; in which men, far from mastering these objects, have become assimilated to them; and in which feelings exist only in so far as they can still be expressed through reification.

As long as the discussion concerned only these first three novels, Robbe-Grillet was anxious to stress an important difference between his fictional world and any Marxist attempt to interpret it as a revolt against dehumanization. Marxists, he said, are people who take up a position, I am a realist, objective writer; I create an imaginary world that I do not judge, that I neither approve nor condemn, but whose existence I record as an essential reality.

Indeed, it was this that constituted Robbe-Grillet's originality within the development of the modern novel, which had long made reification the very centre of artistic creation. Kafka, Sartre in *La Nausée,* Camus in *L'Étranger* still preserved humanist perspectives, explicitly or implicitly, which quite obviously made these books works of absence. Robbe-Grillet's cold world so pushed the observation of absence into the background, on to the implicit level, that it scarcely remained visible to the critic trying to discover the over-all signification of his world.

With *Le Labyrinthe*, the latest of his novels to be published, the human judgement on the world that Robbe-Grillet describes penetrates his work for the first time. From the first page to the last, the feeling of anxiety dominates the work. This is the new element that is added to the themes and formal means that Robbe-Grillet had already discovered and used in his previous works. It is in this sense that this book interests me, as a stage, a link in a chain stretched towards the future, rather than because of its own aesthetic. Robbe-Grillet has shown himself in all his works to be too radical a writer to be content with a human presence reduced to anxiety, a theme that has become almost banal and which he scarcely gives a new signification by inserting it in the empty world of his earlier novels. And so, in his latest work, which is not a book but a film, *L'Année dernière à Marienbad*, he adds to the anxiety its other side, the one that alone enables him to give to human reality in the contemporary world its over-all dimension: hope. It is not that Robbe-Grillet has become an optimist in relation to the values that animate this *oeuvre*, and it is certain that in contemporary society optimism can only be a facile, cheap lie, but in this very society, as in all others, when the problem of authentic human existence is posed, it at first appears as a problem of the nature of time, individual and historic. Robbe-Grillet's first three novels expressed, among other things, the reified character of his world by the elimination of any temporal element. *La Jalousie*, which is the most radical of them, is situated in a continual present. Four chapters out of seven begin with

the word 'now'. One of the modalities by which time can be introduced
into an atemporal world was naturally anxiety. But, as I have already
said, the description of anxiety would have been incomplete without
the addition of the other aspect of temporal experience, of which it is
merely the negative counterpart: hope (real and justified, or illusory
and disappointed). It is a theme that has passed unnoticed by most of
the critics although, as in the novels, it must be sought not at some almost
unattainable depth, but on the simple level of the story, as
immediately recounted in *L'Année dernière à Marienbad*. The baroque
castle of Marienbad is, transposed into film, the same world of
emptiness and death in which nothing can ever happen, in which one
takes part in games that presuppose that the player may lose, but in
which certain others always lose (although the latter are not present in
the film)[9] and in which two individuals still pose the problem of hope.
Hope and anxiety are merely the two subjective aspects of a reality
whose ontological aspect is time, and this is so, not only in its future
dimension, but in all its dimensions, and, implicitly too, in *that of the
past*. On the common-sense level, the problem of knowing whether
something did or did not happen last year is the problem involving the
concordance of indices, evidence, and memories; in Robbe-Grillet's
world, the problem of knowing whether the two protagonists really met
or whether, on the contrary, nothing more happened last year at
Marienbad than pseudo-events devoid of meaning and temporality, like
all those that occur at every moment in the castle, cannot be decided
by any memory or any evidence. Neither a photograph, nor a broken
heel, nor the shared memory of exceptionally cold weather can have
decisive importance. The fact that the man and the women did not
meet last year at Marienbad depends solely on the valid or illusory
character of the hope that still exists in their consciousnesses and whose
reality constitutes the content of the film. If they succeed not only in
leaving the castle but in finding elsewhere (in the terms of the film, in
the garden) an authentic life, a life in which men and human feelings
may really exist, in which events might take place, then it is certain that
they met at Marienbad. If not, neither photographs nor the most
irrefutable evidence will modify in any way the fact that no such
meeting took place. And Robbe-Grillet is too radical a writer to be
unaware that the answer to the problem of the film depends not only
on the will of the two protagonists, but primarily on the nature of the
castle and the nature of the garden. It is what sociologists discovered
long ago when they affirmed the *historical and social* character of the
objective signification of the *affective and intellectual life of
individuals*. And here too Robbe-Grillet is not only a very far-reaching

writer, but also (perhaps it is the same thing) a perfectly honest one. The answer that he gives twice, at the beginning of the film and at the end (though the spectator who sees the film for the first time is scarcely aware of it) is quite unequivocal. The two protagonists have done the best that men living within a society in which we live can do: they have set out towards a different world, in which they will seek life, though with none too clear an idea as to what they mean by it (as they themselves say in the course of the film). They set out towards the garden, which they hope will be a new world for them, a world in which men could be themselves; but they found nothing there, for the garden, like the castle, was only a cemetery:

> The park of this hotel was a kind of garden *à la française* without any trees or flowers, without any foliage . . . Gravel, stone, marble, straight lines, marked out rigid spaces, surfaces without mystery. It seemed, at first glance, impossible to get lost here . . . at first glance . . . down straight paths, between the statues with frozen gestures and the granite slabs, where you were now already getting lost, forever, in the calm of the night, alone with me.[10]

Of course, Robbe-Grillet's *oeuvre* poses many other properly aesthetic problems, but these primarily concern the modifications that the content has brought to the fictional form. It seems to me, however, that this simple analysis of the most immediate content of the writings of Nathalie Sarraute and Robbe-Grillet and of the latter's film is already enough to show that if one gives to the word realism the meaning of creating a world whose structure is analagous to the essential structure of the social reality in which the *oeuvre* has been written, Nathalie Sarraute and Robbe-Grillet are among the most radically realistic writers in contemporary French literature.[11]

NOTES and REFERENCES

1   This study is the text of a paper read at a conference organized in Brussels with Nathalie Sarraute and Alain Robbe-Grillet. To this paper I have added an analysis of Robbe-Grillet's novels published in the review *Médiations* (4: 1962). The contributions by Nathalie Sarraute and Robbe-Grillet were published by the *Revue de Sociologie de L'Université de Bruxelles* (2: 1963).

2   On this subject see Georg Lukács, *History and Class Consciousness* (1971) (trans. R. Livingstone) London: Merlin Press, and Lucien Goldmann, 'La Réification' in *Recherches Dialectiques*, Paris: Gallimard.

3   A decisive step towards a realist literature might be made by a
     writer who would succeed in integrating the two aspects of reality
     recorded with such penetration by Nathalie Sarraute and
     Robbe-Grillet respectively.

4   And which, contrary to what Robbe-Grillet often says of his
     novels, is not strictly situated on the level of the central character,
     but to some extent above him, as with all the classical novelists.

5   This might well be the last external element added to the essential
     content of the novel, though it is much more closely connected
     with this content than were the allusions to the Oedipus myth in
     the preceding work. In relation to the problem of the nature of
     the human world imagined by Robbe-Grillet, a world which, as I
     have said, corresponds very closely to the essence of Western
     industrial society, the fact that the victim was to a certain extent
     a marginal, alien individual, and that her disappearance removed a
     disturbing element, though no doubt important, remains
     nevertheless incidental.

6   Claude Ollier and Jean Catrysse, Professor at the University of
     Caracas, have, independently of each other, drawn my attention
     to the fact that Robbe-Grille's text, far from affirming that
     Mathias did in fact kill the girl, suggests on the contrary doubt
     and the possibility of a purely imaginary crime. This remark seems
     to me to be justified and I now think that, in so far as Mathias
     becomes gradually more aware of the fundamental passivity of the
     world, the reality of his act tends — like that of all acts — to be
     effaced, transforming the act into dream, hullucination, or pure
     imagination. Mathias, who began by killing the girl, ends by no
     longer having killed her and by becoming himself a mere observer.
     On the basis of my analysis of *L'Immortelle*, Anne Olivier has drawn
     my attention to the possibility of a different and complementary
     interpretation of *Le Voyeur, La Jalousie,* and even *L'Année
     dernière à Marienbad*. Indeed, it may be that in these works, and
     in his latest film, Robbe-Grillet wished to contrast a consciousness
     orientated towards the imaginary that it sees and lives with a
     world in which men, having become objects, are unaware of and
     eliminate the imaginary (and in which it remains at most partially
     accessible to children).

     The possible — I would say probable — validity of such an analysis,
     which may even correspond with the conscious intentions of the writer,
     seems to me not only compatible with the reality of the structures
     I have tried to elucidate, but illuminates and complements these
     structures.

     It is, in effect, the totality embracing the human person — the old
     problematic hero reduced to the status of a voyeur of the imaginary —
     and a world homologous with contemporary industrial society,
     whose problems, nature, and laws, Robbe-Grillet has grasped,
     consciously or unconsciously, but in any case in a realistic way,
     that constitutes the world of his works.

     Anne Olivier intends to study the works of Robbe-Grillet from
     this point of view.

7   A modern economist observed the same phenomenon when he remarked that there were no longer any individuals important enough in the economic life for their deaths to affect the Stock Exchange.

8   Alain Robbe-Grillet, *Jealousy* (trans. Richard Howard) (1960) London: Calder and Boyers p. 16.

9   The players who lose being simply the counterpart of the one who wins and possessing no proper reality. Robbe-Grillet was right in this, for those who really lose in life could not enter this film without destroying its unity.

10   Alain Robbe-Grillet, *Last Year at Marienbad* (trans. Richard Howard) (1962) London: Calder p. 151.

11   I hope to publish soon a study of the novels of Claude Ollier that will continue this line of analysis.

4 *L'Immortelle*[1]

Robbe-Grillet's latest film,[2] a work interesting both in itself and for the place it occupies in the intellectual development of a particularly important writer, has just been shown for a week in a small Latin Quarter cinema, after a marked lack of success at the box office.

Though very clear, this film has nevertheless proved to be difficult of access for the average cinema public, which explains its almost total, but let us hope provisional failure, for one day it may well become a classic of the cinema clubs.

In view of the small amount of space at our disposal we shall leave to one side the technical and aesthetic aspects of *L'Immortelle*, concentrating our attention on its content and the place it occupies in the *oeuvre* of the novelist and film-maker.

On an immediate plane, the film recounts a simple enough story. A Frenchman, a *lycée* teacher in Turkey (we shall call him the narrator), remembers in a more or less fragmentary and apparently disordered way an adventure of a more or less sado-masochistic character that he had in that country, whose language he does not know, with a woman whose real name, address, and social background he never knew. She enters like a meteor into his life and disappears as suddenly. After a long, fruitless search, the hero suddenly meets her at a street corner; obviously frightened, she persuades him to get into her car and both set out for a long night drive. Suddenly, in the middle of the road, appears one of the two dogs belonging to an enigmatic man whom we have already seen at various points in the film; terrified, the young woman drives the car straight into a tree and is killed. Later, the narrator tries to understand what happened, his own place in an incomprehensible world in which people speak 'Turkish', the relations between Laïlé and this world, and in the end buys the same car, which he finds in a second-hand dealer's, goes over the same route and is killed in the same circumstances at the very same place as the first accident occurred.

Recounted in so schematic a way, the anecdote may seem banal but, on this web, Robbe-Grillet has taken up once again the problems that dominate all his works and which already structured *L'Année dernière à Marienbad*, those of the relation between the subject, the dehumanized world of reification, and the possibilities of human hope.

In this film Laïlé or Leila (her name is not certain and changes several times in the course of the film) has a very precise function in the over-all structure constituted by these three elements. She is the imaginary dimension, real and unreal at once, that enables the man to realize himself as Man, to affirm himself and – though this is not made explicit in the film – to want something, to hope. Nevertheless, Robbe-Grillet is the opposite of a romantic;[3] he knows that hope, receptivity to the imaginary, is not independent of the real world of everyday life nor simply alien to it. There is between Laïlé and the world an *essential relation*, as enigmatic and incomprehensible as this meaningless world itself. Of this relation, Robbe-Grillet indicates for us only the relevant elements. The world is hostile to the imaginary; it is presented in the form of two enormous threatening dogs who accompany a fat, silent, enigmatic bourgeois, the silent stare of the fisherman by the seashore, the hostile attitude of the workmen in the quarry, all of which create an atmosphere of permanent menace.

Not for an instant is there any doubt that this world is hostile to Laïlé. But she too puts the world in question. When she is present, the houses and battlements become ruins, the mosques cardboard stage sets, the cemeteries and underground passages lies propagated for the benefit of tourists, in short, the world loses its reality. From the beginning of the film, we know that the world and the imaginary are mutually exclusive, incompatible in the long run. The world is made bearable only by the presence of Laïlé, yet that same world, symbolized by the dog that appears in the middle of the road, will finally destroy her.

But is Laïlé really killed physically? And who killed her? In the film, another woman (the maid), who looks like her and who bears the same name, has become so integrated into the world as to be a mere object; a third woman seems to be terrorized and quite unable to express anything; when she speaks, it is to tell the narrator that Laïlé's death was no accident, that she was killed and that he is the murderer. It is this that will drive him to suicide.

In reality, all these apparently contradictory statements are true and complementary. Laïlé was killed by the narrator who failed to protect her presence in the world, but she was also killed by the world, which did not allow the man to reach her. She was and is still being killed everyday by the world in the triple mode of murder (through the arranged accident), of integration into its objectivity, and oppression.

There is much that could be said about the many isolated, highly significant scenes, but it would require more detailed work to do them justice. It should be noted, however, that Robbe-Grillet wished to stress explicitly that the reified and inhuman world in which neither Laïlé nor the narrator is able to live embraces every social stratum; he expresses this first at an important moment in the film, the disappearance of Laïlé, in a scene in which workmen look at her with the same hostility as the bourgeois with the dogs, a scene that is immediately followed by another in which some workmen are carrying a coffin somewhere, probably to a false cemetery.

Indeed, the film has a quite regular, even dialectical structure. It is made up of three almost equal parts (it would not be too much to call them the thesis, antithesis, and synthesis).

The first recounts the appearance of Laïlé, who destroys the world and renders it unreal; when she is there, the walls are in ruin, the palaces destroyed, the fisherman absent, his chair at the sea's edge no longer there, the man without his dogs. Sometimes, it is true, during a reception, men pass in front of her and efface her, but she reappears elsewhere and continues her 'derealizing' action.

In the second part, Laïlé disappears, the process is inverted; the world resumes its reality; the ruined walls are replaced by undamaged fortifications, men begin to speak, but their answers to the narrator's questions are vague and evasive, quite obviously they are avoiding talking about her; it may be that they never knew of the existence of Laïlé, it may be that they did not see the opposition between her and the world, or it may be that they experienced a certain discomfort in remembering her.

In the third and final part, after Laïlé's death, the narrator tries to understand what has happened, his own situation in the whole, and relives in memory earlier scenes, but in a different mode. Whereas in the first part there had been no contact between Laïlé and the world (at most while sleeping on the beach, she had been frightened by barking heard in a dream), the narrator goes over his memories of her, transforming them and correcting them. Now Laïlé and the world are connected – and she finds herself constantly threatened by the world. The underground passage takes on the appearance of a prison tower, the man is reunited with his dogs in a scene in which they in fact did not accompany him in the first part, and soon the narrator sees Laïlé again, imprisoned behind bars, but she disappears as soon as the barking of the dogs is heard. Understanding at last what has happened (and what is still happening every day), namely that the world cannot tolerate the existence of Laïlé, he follows the woman he cannot give up, the woman who gave the film its title, *L'Immortelle*.

Each of the three parts ends with a particularly eloquent and significant scene that should aid our comprehension. The disappearance of Laïlé, which ends the first, is marked by the hostile stares of the quarry workers and by the sight of the coffin; her reappearance, by the walk through a world that quite obviously frightens her, for she now knows its menacing character, and by the final accident. The third part, during which the narrator slowly arrives at an understanding of what has happened and of his own responsibility, ends with his suicide.[4] This is the first appearance of suicide in Robbe-Grillet's work. In what direction will the writer now develop? Romanticism, the affirmation that essence may abandon the world and be situated in the imaginary,[5] a solution towards which a mumber of important contemporary writers are moving? Tragedy, which he came very close to in *L'Immortelle*? A return to the contemplative realism of his first novels, which was content to record implacably the structure of a reified society? Or, lastly, an explicitly humanistic and critical position?[6] One thing is certain; with *L'Immortelle,* Robbe-Grillet finds himself at a turning-point. I would like, if I may, to compare his situation with that of a very different writer, whose preoccupations seem to be of a quite different kind. In his latest play, *Les Séquestrés d'Altona*, Jean-Paul Sartre poses the moral and political problems that have dominated his plays for years and he too arrives for the first time at the suicide of the hero.[7] Here too, the work indicates an analogous turning-point, and here too is posed, though in a quite different way, the problem of later development.

For the sociologist and the historian, the fact that the development of contemporary society has led such different, such contrary writers to the same impasse or, to be more precise, to two such similar impasses, appears to be highly significant.

NOTES and REFERENCES

1   This study was written in colloboration with Anne Olivier.
2   Of which he is both the script-writer and the director. (Alain Robbe-Grillet, *The Immortal One* (a cine-novel, trans. A. M. Sheridan Smith) (1971) London: Calder and Boyars.)
3   So far at least.
4   In fact, the word suicide may be rather strong, for he does not seek death, but tries to be reunited with Laïlé, who is, Robbe-Grillet tells us, 'The Immortal One'.
5   At least the title, *L'Immortelle*, if not the content of the film seems to support this view.
6   Which seems to me unlikely.
7   Hugo's death at the end of *Les Mains sales* is not a suicide but the result of a moral position that is incompatible with life.

5 The Genetic - Structuralist Method in the History of Literature

Genetic structuralist analysis in the *history of literature* is merely the application to this particular field of a *general* method that I believe to be the only valid one in the human sciences. That is to say, I regard cultural creation as a sector, privileged perhaps, but nevertheless of the same nature as all other sectors of human behaviour and, as such, subject to the same laws and offering to scientific study similar, if not identical, difficulties.

In this article, I shall try to analyse some of the fundamental principles of genetic structuralism applied to the human sciences in general and to literary criticism in particular. I shall also develop a few reflections concerning the analogy and opposition between the two great complementary schools of literary criticism that have become associated with this method: Marxism and psychoanalysis.

Genetic structuralism sets out from the hypothesis that *all* human behaviour is an attempt to give a *meaningful response* to a particular situation and tends, therefore, to create a balance between the subject of action and the object on which it bears, the environment. This tendency to equilibrium, however, always retains an unstable, provisional character, in so far as any equilibrium that is more or less satisfactory between the mental structures of the subject and the external world culminates in a situation in which human behaviour transforms the world and in which this transformation renders the old equilibrium inadequate and engenders the tendency to a new equilibrium that will in turn be superseded.

Thus human realities are presented as two-sided processes: *destructuration* of old structurations and *structuration* of new totalities capable of creating equilibria capable of satisfying the new demands of the social groups that are elaborating them.

From this point of view, the scientific study of human facts, whether economic, social, political, or cultural, involves an effort to elucidate these processes by uncovering both the equilibria that they are destroying and those towards which they are moving. Having said this, one has only to become involved in some concrete research to come up against a whole series of problems. I shall try here to say something about the most important of these.

In the first place, there is the problem of knowing who in fact is the *subject* of thought and action. Three types of answer are possible and they involve essentially different attitudes. One may, in effect, like empiricists, rationalists and, more recently, phenomenologists, see this subject in the *individual*; or one may, as in certain types of romantic thought, reduce the individual to a mere epiphenomenon and see in the *collectivity* the only real, authentic subject; or one may as in dialectical, Hegelian, and above all Marxist thought accept, like the romantics, the collectivity as real subject, without forgetting however that this collectivity is no more than a complex network of inter-individual relations and that it is important always to specify the structure of this network and the particular place that the individuals occupy within it — the individuals appearing quite obviously as the immediate, if not ultimate, subjects of the behaviour being studied.

Setting aside the romantic position, which is orientated towards mysticism that denies the individual all reality and autonomy, in so far as it believes that the individual may and must become identified wholly in the totality, the question may be seriously asked as to why the work should in the first place be attached to the social group and not to the individual who wrote it. Such a question is given all the more substance when one considers that the dialectical perspective does not deny the importance of the individual and that the rationalist, empiricist, or phenomenologist positions do not deny the reality of the social environment either, though they see it only as an external conditioning, that is to say, as a reality whose action on the individual has a causal character.[1]

The answer is simple: when it tries to grasp the work in its cultural (literary, philosophical, artistic) specificity, the study that confines its attention solely or primarily to the author may, in the present state of empirical studies, account, *at best*, for its internal unity and the relation between the whole and its parts; but it cannot establish in a positive way a relation *of the same type* between this work and the man who created it. On this plane, if one takes the individual as the subject, most of the work remains accidental and it is impossible to go beyond the level of more or less intelligent and ingenious comment.

For, as I have already said elsewhere, the psychological structure is too complex a reality for one to be able to analyse it with the help of various sets of evidence concerning an individual who is no longer alive, or an author whom one does not know personally, or even on the basis of the intuitive or empirical knowledge of an individual to whom one is bound by close bonds of friendship.

In short, no psychological study can account for the fact that Racine wrote precisely the dramas and tragedies that he did and explain why he could not, in any circumstances, write the plays of Corneille or Moliere.[2]

Now, curious as it may seem, when we are studying great works of culture, sociological study finds it easier to uncover *necessary* links by relating them to collective unities whose structuration is much easier to elucidate.

These unities are no doubt merely complex networks of inter-individual relations, but the complexity of the psychology of individuals derives from the fact that each of them belongs to a fairly large number of different groups (familial, occupational, national, friends and acquaintances, social classes, etc.) and that each of these groups acts upon his consciousness thus helping to form a unique, complex, and relatively incoherent structure, whereas conversely, as soon as we study a sufficiently large number of individuals *belonging to one and the same social group*, the action of other different social groups to which each of them belongs and psychological elements due to this membership cancel each other out, and we are confronted with a much simpler, more coherent structure.[3]

From this viewpoint, the relations between the truly important work and the social group, which – through the medium of the creator – *is, in the last resort, the true subject of creation*, are of the same order as relations between the elements of the work and the work as a whole. In either case, we are confronted by the relations between the elements of a comprehensive structure and the totality of this structure, relations of both a comprehensive and an explanatory kind. That is why, although it is not absolutely absurd to imagine that if the individual Racine had received a different education, or lived in a different environment, he might have been able to write plays like those of Corneille or Molière, it is, on the other hand, absolutely inconceivable that the seventeenth-century *noblesse de robe*[4] should have developed an Epicurean or radically optimistic ideology.

That is to say, in so far as science is an attempt to discover *necessary* relations between phenomena, attempts to relate cultural works with social groups *qua* creative subjects proves – in the present state of our knowledge – much more effective than any attempt to regard the individual as the true subject of creation.

However, once this position has been accepted two problems arise. The first, that of determining what is the order of the relations between the group and the work; the second, that of knowing between which works and which groups relations of this type may be established.

On the first point, genetic structuralism (and more specifically the work of Georg Lukács) represents a real turning-point in the sociology of literature. All other schools of literary sociology, old or contemporary, try in effect to establish relations between the *contents* of literary works and those of the collective consciousness. This method, which may sometimes obtain certain results, in so far as such transferences really do exist, nevertheless presents two major inconveniences:

a) the resumption by the writer of elements of the content of the collective consciousness, or, quite simply of the immediate empirical aspect of the social reality that surrounds him, is almost never either systematic or general and is to be found only at certain points in his work. That is to say, in so far as sociological study is orientated, exclusively or principally, towards the search for correspondences of *content*, it allows the unity of the work to escape, and with it its *specifically literary* character.

b) the reproduction of the immediate aspect of social reality and the collective consciousness in the work is, in general, all the more frequent when the writer possesses less creative force and is content to describe or recount his personal experience without transposing it.

That is why literary sociology orientated towards *content* often has an anecdotal character and proves to be especially effective when it studies *works of average importance* or *literary tendencies*, but gradually loses interest as it approaches the major works of creation.

On this point, genetic structuralism has represented a total change of orientation – its basic hypothesis being precisely that the collective character of literary creation derives from the fact that the *structures* of the world of the work are homologous with the mental structures of certain social groups or is in intelligible relation with them, whereas on the level of content, that is to say, of the creation of the imaginary worlds governed by these structures, the writer has total freedom. The use of the immediate aspect of his individual experience in order to create these imaginary worlds is no doubt frequent and possible but in no way essential and its elucidation constitutes only a useful, secondary task of literary analysis.

In reality, the relation between the creative group and the work generally appears according to the following model: the group constitutes a process of structuration that elaborates in the consciousness of its members affective, intellectual, and practical tendencies towards a coherent response to the problems presented by their relations with nature and their inter-human relations. With few exceptions these tendencies fall far short of effective coherence, in so far as they are, as I said earlier, counteracted in the consciousness of individuals by the fact that each of them belongs to a number of other social groups.

Furthermore, mental categories exist in the group only in the form of tendencies moving towards a coherence I have called a world-view, a view that the group does not therefore create, but whose constituent elements it elaborates (and it alone can elaborate) and the energy that makes it possible to bring them together. The great writer (or artist) is precisely the exceptional individual who succeeds in creating in a given domain, that of the literary (or pictorial, conceptual, musical, etc.) work, an imaginary, coherent, or almost strictly coherent world, whose structure corresponds to that towards which the whole of the group is tending; as for the work, it is, in relation to other works, more or less important as its structure moves away from or close to rigorous coherence.

One can see the considerable difference that separates the sociology of contents and structuralist sociology. The first sees in the work a *reflection* of the collective consciousness, the second sees it on the contrary as *one of the most important constituent elements* of this collective consciousness, that element that enables the members of the group to become aware of what they thought, felt, and did without realizing objectively its signification. One can understand why the sociology of contents proves more effective when dealing with works of average importance, whereas conversely genetic-structuralist literary sociology proves more effective when dealing with the masterpieces of world literature.

At this point, an epistemological problem arises: although *all* human groups act on the consciousness, affectivity, and behaviour of their members, only the action of certain particular, specific groups is able to encourage cultural creation. It is particularly important, therefore, for concrete research to define these groups, in order to know in what direction one's investigations should turn. The very nature of great cultural works indicates what their characteristics ought to be. These works represent, in effect, as I have already said, the expression of world views, that is to say, slices of imaginary or conceptual reality, structured in such a way that, without its being necessary to complete their structure in essence, one can develop them into over-all worlds.

That is to say, this structuration can be attached only to groups *whose consciousness tends to an over-all vision of man*.

From the point of view of empirical research, it is certain that, for a long period, social classes were the only groups of this kind, though the question may be posed as to whether this affirmation is equally valid for non-European societies, for Greco-Roman antiquity and the periods that preceded it, and even perhaps for certain sectors of contemporary society; but once again, I must stress that this is a problem for positive empirical research, and not for the ideological sympathies and antipathies that are so often to be found underlying sociological theories.

In any case, the affirmation of the existence of a link between great cultural works and social groups orientated towards an over-all restructuration of society or towards its preservation eliminates at the outset any attempt to link them to a number of other social groups, notably to the nation, generations, provinces, and family, to mention only the most important. Not that these groups do not act on the consciousness of their members and therefore on that of the writer, but they can explain only certain peripheral elements of the work and not its essential structure.[5] Indeed, the empirical data corroborate this affirmation. Membership of seventeenth-century French society can neither explain nor make comprehensible the work of Pascal, Descartes, and Gassendi, or that of Racine, Corneille, and Molière, to the very extent that these works express different and even opposite views, although their authors all belong to seventeenth-century French society. On the other hand, this common membership may account for certain formal elements common to the three thinkers and the three writers.

After these preliminary considerations, we arrive at the most important problem of all sociological research of a genetic-structuralist type: that of the 'carving up' (*découpage*) of the object. When dealing with the sociology of the economic, social, or political life, this problem is particularly difficult and absolutely essential; one can, in effect, study structures only if one has defined in a more or less rigorous way the set of immediate empirical data that make it up and, conversely, one can define these empirical data only in so far as one already possesses a more or less elaborate hypothesis about the structure that gives them unity.

From the point of view of formal logic, the circle may seem to be insoluble; in practice, it is solved extremely well, as are all circles of this kind, by a series of successive approximations.

One sets out with the hypothesis that one may gather a number of facts into a structural unity, one tries to establish between these facts the maximum number of comprehensive and explanatory relations by trying also to include in them other facts that seem alien to the structure that one is uncovering; in this way, one ends up by eliminating some of the facts with which one set out, adding others, and modifying the initial hypothesis; one repeats this operation by successive approximations until one arrives (this, at least, is the ideal, which is reached to a greater or lesser degree according to the case) at a structural hypothesis that can account for a perfectly coherent set of facts.[6]

When studying cultural creation, one finds oneself, it is true, in a privileged situation as far as the initial hypothesis is concerned. It is, in effect, highly probable that great literary, artistic, or philosophical works constitute coherent significatory structures. The first 'carving up' of the object is therefore, as it were, given at the outset. However, it is important to guard against the temptation to place too absolute a trust in this presupposition. The work may, in effect, contain heterogeneous elements that should be distinguished from its essential unity. Furthermore, although the hypothesis of the unity of the work seems highly probable for truly important works taken in isolation, this probability diminishes considerably when we are dealing with *all the writings of one and the same writer*.

That is why, in concrete research, we must begin with the analysis of each of the writer's works, studying them as far as possible in the order in which they were written.

Such a study will enable us to make provisional groupings of writings on the basis of which we can seek in the intellectual, political, social, and economic life of the period, structured social groupings, in which one can integrate, as partial elements, the works being studied, by establishing between them and the whole intelligible relations and, hopefully, homologies.

The progress of a piece of genetic-structuralist research consists in the fact of delimiting groups of empirical data that constitute structures, relative totalities,[7] in which they can later be inserted as elements in other larger, but similar structures, and so on.

This method has, among others, the double advantage first of conceiving of the whole set of human facts in a unitary manner and, then, of being both *comprehensive* and *explanatory*, for the elucidation of a significatory structure constitutes a process of *comprehension*, whereas its insertion into a larger structure is, in relation to it, a process of *explanation*. Let us take an example; to elucidate the tragic structure of Pascal's *Pensées* and Racine's tragedies is a process of comprehension; to insert them into extremist Jansenism by uncovering the structure of this school of thought is a process of comprehension in relation to the latter, but a process of explanation in relation to the writings of Pascal and Racine; to insert extremist Jansenism into the over-all history of Jansenism is to explain the first and to understand the second. To insert Jansenism, as a movement of ideological expression, into the history of the seventeenth-century *noblesse de robe* is to explain Jansenism and to understand the *noblesse de robe*. To insert the history of the *noblesse de robe* into the over-all history of French society is to explain it by understanding the latter, and so on. Explanation and understanding are not therefore *two* different intellectual processes, but one and the same process applied to two frames of reference.

Lastly, I should like to stress that from this viewpoint – in which the passage from appearance to essence, from the partial, abstract, empirical datum to its concrete, objective signification is brought about by the insertion into relative, structured, and significatory totalities – every human fact may, and even must, possess a certain number of significations, differing according to the number of structures into which it can be inserted in a positive and effective way. Thus, for example, if Jansenism must be inserted, through the mediations already indicated, into seventeenth-century French society, in which it represents a retrograde and reactionary ideological current opposed to the progressive historical forces represented above all by the bourgeoisie and the monarchy and, on the ideological plane, by Cartesian rationalism, it is just as legitimate and necessary to insert it into the over-all structure of Western society as it has developed up to our own time, in which case it becomes progressive in the sense that it constitutes one of the first steps in the direction of superseding Cartesian rationalism towards dialectical thinking; and, of course, these two significations, are neither exclusive nor contradictory.

To end, I should like to say something about two particularly important problems in the present state of literary criticism:

a) that of the insertion of literary works into two real and complementary totalities, which may provide elements of understanding and explanation, namely, the individual and the group and

b) on this basis, that of the function of cultural creation in the life of men.

On the first point we have today two scientific schools of a genetic structuralist type corresponding to the attempts to insert works into collective structures and into individual biography: Marxism and psychoanalysis.

Leaving to one side the difficulties already referred to, the difficulties of uncovering individual structures, let us begin by considering these two schools on the methodological plane. Both offer to understand and explain human facts by insertion into the structured totalities respectively of the collective life and of the individual biography. They thus constitute related and complementary methods and the results of each of them ought, to all appearances at least, strengthen and complement those of the other.

Unfortunately, *qua* genetic structuralism, psychoanalysis, at least in the form elaborated by Freud,[8] is not sufficiently consistent and is much too tainted with the scientism that dominated university life at the end of the nineteenth and the beginning of the twentieth centuries. This becomes abundantly apparent on two most important points.

Firstly, in Freudian explanations, the temporal dimension of the future is entirely lacking, and in the most radical way. Under the influence of the determinist scientism of his time, Freud entirely neglects the positive forces of equilibration that act in every human structure, whether individual or collective; for him, to explain is to go back to the experiences of childhood to repressed instinctive forces, while he entirely neglects the positive assumption that consciousness and the relation with reality might have.[9]

Secondly, the individual is, for Freud, an absolute subject for whom other men can only be *objects* of satisfaction or frustration; this fact is perhaps the basis of the absence of future that I have just mentioned.

It would no doubt be false to reduce, in too narrow a way, the Freudian libido to the sexual domain; nevertheless, it is always *individual* and, in Freud's view of mankind, the collective subject and the satisfaction that collective action may bring to the individual are entirely lacking.

One might develop at length with the aid of many concrete examples, the distortions that these perspectives create in Freudian analyses of cultural and historical facts. From this point of view, Marxism seems to me incomparably more advanced, in so far as it integrates not only the future as an explanatory factor but also the individual signification of human facts side by side with their collective signification.

Lastly, on the level that concerns us here, that of cultural works and particularly literary works, it seems to me incontestable that these works may be validly integrated into significatory structures of an individual type and of a collective type. Only, and this goes without saying, the real and valid signification that these two integrations may uncover are at the same time of a different and complementary nature.

The integration of works into individual biography can in effect reveal only their individual signification and their relation with the biographical and psychical problems of the author. That is to say, whatever the validity and scientific rigour of researches of this type might be, they must necessarily situate the work outside its own cultural and proper aesthetic context, and place it at the same level as all the individual symptoms of a particular patient treated by the psychoanalyst.

Supposing — and I would not concede this — that one may validly relate on the individual plane Pascal's writings to his relations with his sister or those of Kleist to the relations with his sister and his father, *one would have brought out an affective and biographical signification in these writings, but one would not have dealt with, or even approached, their philosophical or literary signification.* Thousands and tens of thousands of individuals have certainly had similar relations with members of their family and I cannot see how a psychoanalytical study of these symptoms could in any sense account for the difference *of nature* between the writings of any neurotic and the *Pensées* or *Prinz Friedrich von Homburg*.

The only use, and it is a slight one, of psychological and psychoanalytical analyses for literary criticism seems to me to be in explaining why in a given concrete situation in which a given social group has elaborated a certain world-view a particular individual happens, on account of his individual biography, to be particularly capable of creating a conceptual or imaginary world, in so far as, among other satisfactions, he could also find in it a derivative or sublimated satisfaction for his own unconscious aspirations.[10] This means that it is only on the basis of a historico-sociological analysis that the philosophical signification of the *Pensées*, the literary and the aesthetic signification of Kleist's plays, and the genesis of each may be *understood as cultural facts*.

Psychological studies may at most help us to understand why, among hundreds of Jansenists, it was precisely Racine and Pascal who were able to express the tragic vision on the literary and philosophical plane without, however, providing any information (except of a secondary and unimportant kind) concerning the nature, content, and signification of this expression.

It only remains to me now to touch, somewhat schematically, on a particularly important problem: that of the individual function (games, dreams, morbid symptoms, sublimations) and the collective function (literary, cultural, and artistic values) of the imaginary, in relation to the human significatory structures that all possess the common characteristics of being dynamic and structured relations between a subject (collective or individual) and an environment.

The problem is a complex and little studied one, and I can do no more, in ending this article, than formulate a vague and provisional hypothesis. It seems to me in effect that, on the psychical plane, the action of the subject is always presented in the form of a set of aspirations, tendencies, desires, whose complete satisfaction is prevented by reality.

Marx and Lukács on the collective plane, Piaget on the individual plane, have closely studied the modifications that the difficulties and obstacles raised by the objects introduce into the very nature of these desires and aspirations. Freud has shown that, on the individual plane, desires, even in a modified form, may be content with a partial satisfaction and accept repression. His great merit lies in having discovered that the rational relation with reality requires as a complement an imaginary satisfaction, capable of assuming the most varied forms, from the adapted structures of the lapsus and the dream to the non-adapted structures of insanity.

Despite all the differences (I do not believe that there can be a collective unconscious), it may be that the function of culture is analogous. Human groups can act rationally on reality and adapt themselves to the frustrations and partial satisfactions imposed by this action and by the obstacles it encounters, only in so far as rational and transforming action is accompanied by complete satisfactions on the level of conceptual or imaginary creation.

It should also be added that although, on the individual plane, repressed instincts survive *in the unconscious* and tend towards a symbolic satisfaction that is always a *possession of the object*, collective tendencies, which are often implicit but not unconscious, are aimed not at a *possession* but at the *realization of a coherence*.

Cultural creation thus compensates for the mixture and compromises that reality imposes on subjects and facilitates their insertion into the real world, which is perhaps the psychological basis of catharsis.

A hypothesis of this kind, which would integrate without difficulty what is valid in Freudian analysis and in Marxist studies of art and cultural creation, might account both for the kinship — so often suspected by many theoreticians — and the difference of nature that nevertheless survives between, on the one hand, the game, the dream, and even certain forms of morbid imagination and, on the other hand, the great literary, artistic, and even philosophical creations.

May 1964

The hypothesis formulated in the first study of this volume leads me to add a few reflections to the methodological writings concerning the sociology of culture that I have published so far and, particularly, to the present study.

It has proved, in effect, that the relation between the work and the social structure with which it is associated is much more complex in capitalist society, and notably in the case of the literary form that is most closely associated with the economic sector of this society, the novel, than in the other literary or cultural creations examined in my previous studies.

In these studies, my research led me to the hypothesis that the work is situated at the meeting-point between the highest forms of the tendencies to coherence proper to the collective consciousness and the highest forms of unity and coherence of the individual consciousness of the creator.

Important cultural works could no doubt have a critical, even oppositional, character in relation to the over-all society in so far as they are associated with a social group oriented towards such a critical and oppositional character in relation to society as a whole. Having said this, cultural creation was nonetheless always based upon a close coincidence between the structure and the values of the collective consciousness and the structures and values of the work.

However, this situation becomes much more complex in a market society, in capitalist society, where the existence and development of an economic sector has precisely as a consequence a tendency to the disappearance or, at least, a reduction in the status of the collective consciousness as mere reflection.

In this case, the literary work can no longer be based on the total or almost total coincidence with the collective consciousness and is situated in a rather different dialectical relationship with the class with which it is associated.

In the case of the traditional novel, with a problematic hero, I have already shown that the homology is limited to the over-all structure of the world described in the novel and to the values of the individual, the autonomy and development of the personality, which correspond to the structure of exchange and to the explicit values of liberalism. Having said this, it is precisely in the name of these same explicit values alone, which still structure the consciousness of the bourgeoisie in its ascendant and later liberal periods (whereas this same consciousness reduces to the implicit all trans-individual values), that the novelist is opposed to a society and a social group that necessarily deny in practice the values that they implicitly affirm. Moreover, the novel with a problematic hero is, by its very structure, critical and realistic; it observes and affirms the impossibility of basing an authentic development other than on the trans-individual values of which the society created by the bourgeoisie has precisely suppressed all authentic, overt expression. I should remark in passing that this leads on the whole – and apart from a few exceptions, of course – to a break with the individualistic philosophy which, in its various forms (rationalist, empiricist, and synthetic in the philosophy of the Enlightenment), accepts and assumes the world constituted by the individual, autonomous consciousnesses whose authenticity the novel brings into question. Let me add that this complex structuration of the relations between society and literary creation is perhaps made possible by a society that explicitly affirms the value of the critical individual consciousness independent of any external attachment and which was able by that very fact to increase the degree of autonomy enjoyed by such an individual consciousness.[11]

The later development of capitalism, with the two principal turning-points mentioned in the first study in this book, namely:

a) the passage to an economy of monopolies and trusts and, on the literary plane, to the novel of the dissolution of the character and

b) the development of a capitalism of organization and a consumer society, and the appearance of the new novel and a theatre centred on absence and the impossibility of communication, again alters to a certain extent the relation that concerns us here. For the concomitant disappearances on the one hand, of the individualistic, liberal ideology in the economy and, on the other, of the character and its search in the novel, suppress the principal common element that still survived between the collective consciousness and literary creation, thus emphasizing the oppositional and critical character of such creation.

In the second phase in the history of bourgeois society, the phase that Marxists have called the crisis of capitalism and which was characterized by the existence of unstable and temporary equilibria, periodically re-established by extremely violent social and political crises following one another at short intervals (World War I, the Russian revolution, the revolutionary crises of 1917–1923 in Europe, Italian Fascism, the extremely widespread economic crisis of 1929–1933, the rise of Nazism, World War II), philosophical thought, which also abandoned the unchallenged value of the autonomous individual consciousness and sought a basis in the concepts of limit, anxiety, and death, links up in existentialism with the most important development in literary creation. The relation between the novels of Kafka and existentialist thought has often been stressed and, in France, Sartre and Camus were both philosophical thinkers and writers.

Lastly, in the contemporary period, the rebirth of an ahistorical and non-individualistic rationalism centred on the idea of permanent and invariable structures and the appearance of the most recent forms of the literary avant-garde create a complex situation that is difficult to formulate without embarking on a deeper analysis of both sectors of reality.

Nevertheless, it should be stressed that, from the point of view of literary creation, the most important phenomenon seems to me to be the disappearance of that social stratum, of individuals who played an active and responsible role in the economic, social, and political life, and therefore in the cultural life — a role which, though theoretically open to all as a universal right, was in fact the privilege of a limited group (which became still further reduced in the imperialist period compared with the period of liberal capitalism).

The consumer societies have considerably increased the distribution of cultural works through what sociologists call the *mass media* (radio, television, cinema), to which has recently been added the paperback book.[12] But the nature of the reading of books and the hearing of plays has essentially altered, for it is obviously very different to read a book or listen to a play, accepting or rejecting it, but remaining nevertheless in discussion and intellectual communication with it, and to remain at the level of passive consumption, entertainment, and leisure.

Here too, with the disappearance of the social stratum that participated most actively in the elaboration of a collective consciousness, the writer finds himself confronted by a society that consumes a much greater mass of goods, including his own works, than ever before, a society that therefore provides a few privileged writers with a particularly high standard of living, but which can no longer help them at the level of creation except in a very minor way.

If we are to elucidate these problems, a great deal of particularly urgent empirical research must be undertaken, especially into the nature of reading and participation in theatrical events (it is characteristic that Proust speaks of 'hearing La Berma', whereas today we find it more natural to say that we 'see' a great actor) and also into the relations between creators and the relatively small group of individuals who, in contemporary society, have access to decision-making in the economic, social, and political spheres.

In the meantime, I have tried to formulate a few remarks much more

with a view to raising a number of problems than to providing
solutions.[13]

NOTES and REFERENCES

1   From this point of view, a sociological study, may at most, help
    to explain the genesis of the work, but it cannot in any sense
    contribute to its *understanding.*
2   However, although it is impossible to insert into the biographical
    structure content and form, in short, the properly literary,
    philosophical, or artistic structure of great cultural works, a
    psychological school of a genetic-structuralist type,
    psychoanalysis, does succeed to a certain extent in uncovering
    side be side with this specific cultural essence a structure and an
    individual signification for these works, which it believes can be
    inserted into the biographical development. I shall return briefly
    at the end of this article to the possibilities and limits of such an
    insertion.
3   Indeed, empirical statistics are aware of the analogous
    consequences of the same factor; it is practically impossible to
    predict without a wide margin of error whether Tom, Dick, or
    Harry will marry, have a car accident, or die the following year,
    but it is not difficult, on the other hand, to predict with very little
    margin of error the number of marriages, accidents, deaths that
    will take place in France in a given week in the year.
        Having said this, and although we are dealing with related
    phenomena, there are considerable differences between these
    statistical forecasts, concerning a reality whose structures have not
    been uncovered, and genetic-structuralist analysis.
4   People who owed their patents of nobility to administrative or
    legal posts they or their ancestors had bought (Tr.).
5   Sociological studies of this kind are situated on the same level as
    the sociology of content which, also, can account only for certain
    secondary or incidental elements in works of art.
6   By way of example, one might begin with the hypothesis of the
    existence of a significatory structure that we will call dictatorship;
    in the end, one would group together a set of phenomena like, for
    example, political régimes in which the government enjoys
    absolute power; but if one tries to account by means of a single
    structural hypothesis for the genesis of all these régimes, one
    would soon see that dictatorship is not a significatory structure
    and that one must distinguish between groups of dictatorship that
    are of quite different natures and have quite different
    significations; whereas, for example, the concepts of revolutionary
    dictatorship or, on the contrary, postrevolutionary Bonapartist
    dictatorship do seem to constitute operational concepts.
        Similarly, any attempt to make a unitary interpretation of the
    writings of Pascal (and there are a number of them) fail when
    confronted by the fact that his two most important works *Les*

Provinciales and the *Penseés* express essentially different points of view. One must, if one is to understand them, regard them as expressions of two distinct, though in certain respects related, structures.

7 On this level, above all in the sociology of culture, it is useful to employ an external and quantitative 'rail'. If one is interpreting a written work, it goes without saying that one may have a number of different interpretations that account for sixty to seventy per cent of the text. That is why one ought not to regard such a result as scientific confirmation. On the other hand, it is rare to find two different interpretations that integrate eighty to ninety per cent of the text, and the hypothesis that leads one there is likely to be a valid one. This probability increases considerably if one manages to insert the structure uncovered in genetic analysis into a greater totality, if one manages to use it in an effective way for the explanation of other texts one had not at first been concerned with and especially if, as was the case in my study of seventeenth-century tragedy, one manages to elucidate and even to predict a number of facts unknown to specialists and historians.

8 I know too little about its later developments to speak of them with any authority.

9 It would no doubt be tempting to explain this characteristic of Freud's work by the fact that he was a doctor and studied above all sick people, that is to say, people in whom the forces of the past and repressions predominated over the positive forces orientated towards balance and the future. Unfortunately, the criticism that I have just formulated also applies to Freud's philosophical and sociological studies.

   The word 'future' is to be found in the title of only one of his writings and, typically, the work is called 'The Future of an Illusion'. Furthermore, the content of this work shows that this future does not exist.

10 Conversely, sociological study can provide no information as to the biographical and individual signification of works of art and can provide psychoanalysts only with relatively secondary information as to the forms of real or imaginary satisfaction of individual aspirations, which, at a given period and in a given society, the collective structures encourage or impose.

11 A particularly complex situation may occur, for example, in cases when the critical attitude and the opposition of the individual towards the over-all collective mentality themselves constitute values advocated by certain partial sectors of this mentality.

12 Which constitutes, as I have already said elsewhere, a sort of encyclopedia, without any values or characteristics of its own, whose appearance seems to me homologous with the rebirth of a non-individualistic rationalism.

13 I developed these ideas for the first time, in a rather less schematic way, in a text that UNESCO will publish in 1966, as a working document to be used in the course of an investigation into new values and forms in artistic creation.

Index

Abdul Hamid, pan-Islamism, 112 , 113, 114
Adamov, 13
Aeschylus, 85
artist, the, a problematic individual opposed to society, 15

Bakunin, Mikhail, 98
Balzac, Honoré de, 16n. 3; literary expression of a world as structured by bourgeois values, 13-14; creation of great literary universe, 14, 17 n. 9; analysis of psychology of the character, 133-4
Beckett, Samuel, 13
best-sellers, relation to new forms of collective consciousness, 15
bourgeois society, creation of absolute values from its own conscious values (individualism, thirst for power, money, eroticism), 11, 12, 14, 15; the novel as a form of resistance to, 13; failure to create a literary form expressing its real consciousness (Balzac excepted), 14; a radically profane and ahistorical ideology, 14; first radically non-aesthetic form of consciousness, 14-15; ignores existence of art, 15; opposed by Tolstoy, 62; 'crisis of capitalism' phase of development (Marx), 168-9

Camus, Albert, 169; 'philosophy of the absurd', 6; L'Étranger, 6, 139, 147
capitalism, Western, 64, 107, 122-3; division between 1920s and today's reorganization, 123; transformation from liberal character to imperialism, 135, 136, 138; differentiated from earlier forms of social organization, 136; increasing independence of objects, 138; and the relation between a cultural work and its social structure, 167; later developments, 168-9

Cartesian rationalism, progress towards dialectical thinking, 163
Catholic Church, in Les Noyers de l'Altenburg, 111
Catryse, Jean, and Le Voyeur, 150 n. 6
Cervantes, Miguel de, Don Quixote, a novel of chivalry, 2, 3, 16 n. 3; external mediating agent, 4; character of its ending, 4, 50; its hero, 5, 30, 138
Chateaubriand, François, vicomte de, 85
Chiang Kai-shek, 72, 80; in La Condition humaine, 64, 65, 67, 68, 128 n. 21
China, crisis in her culture, 25-6; differentiated from Western industrialized countries, 37; Communist policy, 64; struggle against imperialism 95; effect of permanent civil war, 122; in La Condition humaine, 64, 67-8, 107; in Les Conquérants, 36
Christian person, total integration of the individual, 86; conflict with communism, 97
communism, influence on M., 35-6; only authentic reality in a declining world, 35; ideology of two opposing groups, 63-4; 'permanent revolution', v. 'socialism in one country', 64, 128 n. 23; reality of its acceptance for socialist intellectuals, 107; represented in La Condition humaine, 64-6; in Les Conquérants, 38, 45
Communist International defended by M., 63; differentiated from policy defended by Trotsky, 63-4, 128 n. 23; defeat of problematic community, 83
Communist Party, M.'s acceptance, 83-4, 87; comparison between Le Temps du Mépris and L'Espoir, 83; a non-problematic community, 83; opposition to spontaneity, 83; adopts policy of antifascist struggle (post-

groups, x, xi, 157; continuance under a reified society, 10; conditions for its validity, 14; relationship with history of W. industrial societies, 123; subject to same laws and influences as other aspects of human behaviour, 156; collective unities linking them together, 158, 170 n. 3; encouragement by certain specific groups, 160; characteristics of great works, 160; failure of their unitary study, 162, 170 n. 6; analysis of individual works, 162; function in life of man, 163; disappearance of a socially privileged, limited group, 169; effect of the consumer society, 169

Dadaists, 126 n. 7

death, position in Christian ideology of Middle Ages, 31; subordinate to that of salvation, 31; central philosophical problem in 20th C. crisis of individualism, 31-2; idea involving neither compensation nor atonement (*Les Conquérants*), 43, 124; incompatible with action, 50; loss of primordial significance in a world governed by supra-individual values, 86; man and, 119, 120; two different aspects for M.'s heroes, 124, 126 n. 17

Defoe, Daniel, an isolated individual confronted by world of objects (*Robinson Crusoe*), 138

Dostoievsky, Fyodor, 85, 138; *The Eternal Husband*, 3, 4

Dumas, Alexandre, 15

Eastern society, decline of specific values, 25

economic crisis, 1929-33, sociopolitical consequences, 122, 168

economic life, replacement of qualitative aspects of persons and objects by mediatized and degraded relation, 7, 11; orientation towards exchange values, 8; fringe position of creators, 8, 11-12; transformation into literary life, 10; and the collective consciousness, 11-12; supersession of free enterprise by monopolies and cartels, 12, 135; and bourgeois society, 14; on level of individual consciousness, 137;

assumption of new properties (exchange value and price) by inert objects, 137

Ehrenburg, Ilya, joins Communist Party, 84

Enver Pasha (Young Turk), represents a supranational ideology (Ottomanism), 113, transposition to Stalin, 114; seizure of power in 1917, 131 n. 41; in *Les Noyers de l'Altenburg*, 112-13

eroticism, 48-9; comparison with historical action and reality, 49; resulting nothingness and impotence, 49; as a theme in *La Voie royale*, 55, 72; superseded by love in *La Condition humaine*, 72; connection with domination, 79

L'Espoir, 29, 86, 124; lyrico-epic form, 19, 84-5, 105, 130 n. 32; and communism, 35, 83, 92-3, 127 n. 20; conflict between discipline and revolutionary impetus, 83, 93, 94, 120 n. 20; identification of central struggle-Communist/Fascist Parties, 93, 94; abstract collective character, 94; anarchist/communist conflict, 95, 97-8, 98-9, Stalinist point of view, 95, 96-7; valorization of leadership, 96; sense of virile fraternity, 100; coherence between over-all vision and lives of characters, 103; inhibitory presence of eroticism, love and family, 103-4; world of the novel, 104, 105; and the individual, 105 (characterization), *Garcia*, communist, famous phrase on 'best that a man can do', 95-6; view of political leaders, 96; and Hernandez, 97-8, 98-9; on just wars, 102; and women, 103-4; *Hernandez*, Christian revolutionary, 97-8, 98-9; *Manuel*, conversion to political leader, 96, 98, 100-102; last thoughts, 104-5; (collectives), *anarchists*, courageous and undisciplined, 94, 97-8, 102; *communists*, over-all efficient, 94, 97-8; *Catholics*, hampered by conscience, 94, 98, 102

Europe, revolutionary crises, 1917-23, 168

European Left, repercussion of Nazi seizure of power, 84; and German-Soviet Pact, 1939, 108

exchange value, substitute for use value, 7; focus of economic life, 8;